CW00591023

—

# CHURCH BUILDING

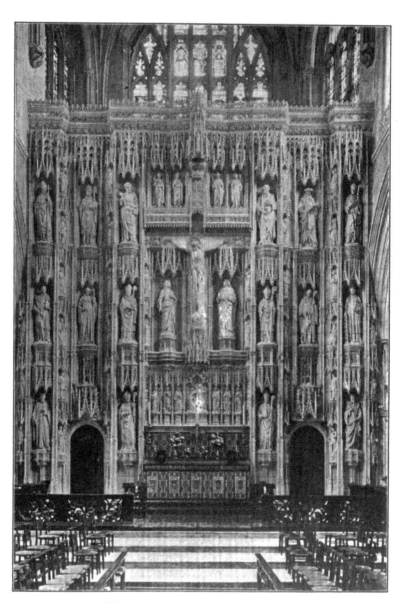

THE REREDOS—WINCHESTER CATHEDRAL.

# CHURCH BUILDING

## A STUDY OF THE
## PRINCIPLES OF ARCHITECTURE
## IN THEIR RELATION TO
## THE CHURCH

By

RALPH ADAMS CRAM

Litt.D., F.A.I.A., F.R.G.S.

SECOND EDITION

BOSTON
SMALL, MAYNARD & COMPANY
MCMXIV

ν

*Copyright 1899, 1900, by*
*Ralph Adams Cram*

———

*Copyright 1901, 1914, by*
*Small, Maynard & Company*
( *Incorporated* )

———

*Entered at Stationers' Hall*

HARVARD COLLEGE LIBRARY
GIFT OF THE
HARVARD CLUB OF BOSTON

MAY 21 1928

*The University Press, Cambridge, U. S. A.*

✠

To the Memory of

CHARLES  FRANCIS  WENTWORTH

✠

# PREFACE TO SECOND EDITION

THE fact that a new printing of this volume is necessary would be evidence in a way that interest has not flagged during the last decade, either in churches or their construction, if evidence were needed. Nothing of the kind is necessary, however, for the fact is patent to every one that concrete religion means more in the world to-day than it has meant for many generations, and that the interest in church building has extended far beyond the architectural profession and has now come to include, in a very special and unusual way, clergy and laity alike. Nor is this interest either technical or archæological: it is not even wholly æsthetic; it is rather a showing forth of a deeper consciousness of the eternal and indispensable nature of the Christian religion itself, of the part it must play in the building up of a new civilization, and of the fact that if it is to do this, it must be, in a measure at least, through the agency of a sane and beautiful art.

A re-reading of this volume bears fruit at least in one way, in that it enforces the truth of the above statements. Were it to be re-written afresh much that appears would be omitted, for it is now but the commonplace of both architect and layman. And yet, fifteen years ago it was necessary to declare these very commonplaces, to lay stress on the most rudimentary principles, to argue even, not only for Gothic as an apposite and a living style, but also for the very principles and ideals that Gothic was once devised to set forth. Now this is no longer necessary, for both have won their position, and in this fact, even more than in the wide development of religious art in the last few years, lies the great encouragement of those who are striving to preserve not alone the art, but the religion, of a great epoch of Christian civilization.

So far as the art itself is concerned, its notable advance owes as little to the schools as did its earliest inception in the first half of the nineteenth century. To this day schools of architecture are generally as scornful both of the problem and its stylistic expression as they ever have been since official architectural schools came into existence. Whatever has been gained has been without their aid, and simply because, schools or no schools, there was a new spirit working in the world, a new demand that inevitably produced the corresponding supply. There is nothing self-conscious in the religious art of the time, nothing factitious or premeditated; it is working instinctively though slowly, and it is gradually reaching out through all classes and all denominations. Little by little it is acquiring coherency, and when once this synthesis is accomplished, it may be able to rise to its high possibilities and materially aid in the achievement of that same coherency and synthesis in the organic forms of the religion it serves, as in the natural forms, which are architecture and all the arts when called into this service.

R. A. C.

March, 1914.

# PREFACE

THE greater portion of the contents of this book appeared originally in serial form in the columns of *The Churchman*. The interest in the work manifested by the public, at and since the time of its original publication, has seemed to the author a justification for its appearance in more permanent form. As here printed, the chapters have been carefully revised and somewhat enlarged, and a number of new illustrations have been included.

The thanks of the author are due to *The Churchman* for courtesies and to the Bates and Guild Company for the use of many valuable illustrations not otherwise accessible.

R. A. C.

# CONTENTS

# ILLUSTRATIONS

# ILLUSTRATIONS

# ILLUSTRATIONS

# ILLUSTRATIONS

# ILLUSTRATIONS

# CHURCH BUILDING

# INTRODUCTION

Art is the measure of civilization. We may assert such claims as we choose, if we have not an art that is instinctive, the natural expression of a healthy people, then we protest in vain. We do not possess a genuine, vital civilization.

Not that we must be able to boast of men so great in the various fields of art that they have won for their names an earthly immortality. Such are rather a sign of a time without art than of one wherein art is universal. The great painters of Venice came just as that brilliant epoch of civilization was swerving toward its fall. Turner was born in the dark ages of modern England. Wagner and Brahms were as voices crying in the wilderness. There have always been dazzling personalities that flashed out of the surrounding gloom like the writing on the wall at the great king's feast; but they are not manifestations of healthy art. They are phenomena. The sanest, most wholesome art is that which is the heritage of all the people, the natural language through which they express their joy of life, their achievement of just living; and this is civilization,— not commercial enterprise, not industrial activity, not the amassing of fabulous wealth, not increase of population or of empire. These may accompany civilization, but they do not prove it.

Since the beginnings of recorded history, art has existed in varying degrees of nobility, but no period has ever come during which it has been essentially wrong, not even the last years of the Roman Empire or the Dark Ages of Europe,— no period until our own; and, whatever it may signify, we are compelled to confess that, when instinctive art had dribbled away in the futilities of Georgian and our own Colonial work, a time came when, so far as art was concerned, we stood below the Navajo Indians and the Maories of New Zealand.

Europe was not much better off, but there was a sufficient difference for the Centennial to give us a vigorous shock; and at once we here in America set ourselves to the task of creating the art that was then considered only one of the amenities of civilization. We did not succeed in making it instinctive; but we learned much, and began a course of imitation that was often most intelligent, while trained specialists succeeded with infinite labor in giving us what, three centuries ago, a common workman would have done without thought and without pains.

We have not realized as yet that art is a result, not a product, and that the conditions we now offer are not such as make it inevitable. When we change the conditions, the art will follow,—not until then.

Art is the result of beautiful ideas, of beautiful modes of life, of beautiful environment. He would be a courageous optimist who would say these existed now in secular life; but it is just because they *do* exist in one place, or can, if we will, that these papers are written.

For our true industrial art, our noble civil architecture, our beautiful dwellings, our great secular pictures,—except for the sporadic cases that owe their existence to isolated genius,—we must wait for different times; but what of the Church? Here is a society within a society, a life that in theory has preserved or reasserted the beautiful ideas and environment that once characterized all phases of life. Surely, if there is any power in the world to-day capable of evoking a vital art, demanding art as her true means of outward expression, it is the Church.

But this is not the case, if we are to judge from results; for the Church here in America does not stand a degree higher than secular powers in her artistic expressions. In fact, she seems even to fall behind. She has created no religious painter, no music, no school of art work, and, above all, no logical architecture. In worldly affairs it has become the fashion to affect the splendors of elaborate architectural form, and the results are as chaotic as one could ask. Style follows style, as fashion changes, until at last we are confronted by an absolutely futile confusion. Has the Church stood aloof from this Babel of tongues? Has she pursued her way uninfluenced by the fads around her? By no manner of means: every newly discovered style has found favor in her eyes; and she has become, architecturally, but the echo of the artificiality of secular life.

It is not surprising that this should be so. Had the life of the Church been unbroken by conflict, had she remained united, she would have maintained her position as the leader, the creator of art; and, under her inspiration and control, painting and sculpture and architecture might easily have continued their development, handing on to secular life the styles and modes they had developed under the spiritual. This was always the case in the past, since Christianity first became dominant. Art in all its forms owed its inspiration to the Church, and without her could not have existed. There is no reason to suppose that there would have been any change, had the Reformation never taken place, or had it been a movement that contented itself with internal reforms, not one that insisted upon revolution and disruption.

Under the circumstances, art as a universal mode of expression, as a common heritage of all men, received its death-blow in the sixteenth century, when the Church was shattered and her power destroyed. From that moment the decadence began; and the fall was swift, indeed, not only in England, but throughout Europe, and chaos took the place of order, uncertainty and affectation that of the clearly defined motives that until then had been followed consistently.

Architecture, together with all art, is the exact expression of the mental, social, and spiritual temper of the times that produce it. That modern secular architecture should be what it is is eminently fitting, but that the same qualities of trivial fashion and triumphant individualism should obtain in a portion of that Church which we hold to be changeless and stable, resting serene above the vacillations and vicissitudes of human society, is certainly a most unfortunate condition of things.

The results of recent church building in America are such that it is impossible for us to deny that the principles upon which we work are radically wrong. They may voice the chaos of contemporary social and economic conditions, but they slander the nature of the immutable Church.

That this should be so is by no means surprising. The Anglican Church was established in America at precisely the worst time in the history of this branch of the Catholic Church, and therefore the time when its architecture was at the lowest ebb. Severed almost entirely from the parent stem, it was cut off from all the growing influences that were to re-create something of early vigor and glory in the mother Church, and was left defenceless in the midst of the rushing social events and political conditions that were to show their general effect through the collapse of all local and national art.

During the seventeenth and eighteenth centuries the neo-pagan style, which had gradually lost what shreds of Christian tradition it retained under Wren, served fairly well for the Puritan meeting-houses and for the very few new structures demanded by the prostrate Church; but when the Catholic revival of the first half of the present century began to lead men to desire something more in harmony with church history and tradition than the Georgian pseudo-temples with a steeple on one end and a little, screened chancel on the other, the resulting attempts in this country at a Gothic restoration, in echo of the similar successful restoration in England, were not crowned with striking success. Study of mediæval models rarely went further than the contours of mouldings and the outlines of arches. The old meeting-house principle remained; and flimsy columns of iron, glaring light, awkward galleries, and box pews made Gothic details of no avail. Men bowed before the rocky masses of Durham and in the mysterious caverns of Cologne, but the traditions of the meeting-house and the commands of the wardens and vestry were heavy upon the builders; and though they put jig-sawed tracery in their pointed windows and filled them with ground glass in diamond panes, though they designed wonderful buildings with aisles and transepts, arcades of plaster arches on iron columns, and with beautiful Early English mouldings on their black walnut pews and galvanized iron crockets on their wooden spires, all was of no effect; and the shocking building remained a meeting-house still, only less honorable, less respectable than the Georgian structures of the eighteenth century.

The idea of the architectural restoration in England had taken root, but the growth was wilful and lifeless. Forms were copied after a fashion, but principles were ignored. Therefore, the alleged "Gothic" was an affectation without reality or truth. The false and deadly principles that obtained in church building during the bald eighteenth century persisted obstinately; and, so long as they endured, just so long was good art out of the question.

In England the Catholic and Gothic restorations have succeeded at last in getting back to basic principles; and, as a result, the only vital, modern, consistent church building to-day is that of England. It is based on a clear conception of the nature of a church, and we must accept this in America if we are to see our own church architecture take its place with that of England.

What, then, are the qualities of a church, and their order of precedence? It seems to me that they are four, and that they stand in the following order of importance: —

First of all, a church is a house of God, a place of His earthly habitation, wrought in the fashion of heavenly things, a visible type of heaven itself. From the day when God gave to Solomon the plan and the fashion of the temple down to those wherein our own forefathers lavished their scanty wealth and toiled with devout hands to raise the awful fabrics of the mediæval cathedrals and abbeys, this thought has lain as the corner-stone of every one of the great and splendid churches that brighten Christendom with the memory of devout and reverend times. They were building a house of God, and the treasure and labor lavished so abundantly were consecrated as they might never be on any other structure. All the wonders of art,— the handmaid of religion,— all the treasures gathered from many lands, were lavished here in gratitude and praise and thanksgiving; and nothing was too precious, indeed, all things failed in a measure, to show the deep devotion of faithful men, and their solemn knowledge of the majesty of that Presence that should enter and dwell therein.

There is scant kinship between this spirit and that which prompts and governs the construction of contemporary churches. Were it restored, if only in a small measure, men would understand more clearly the fatal error of the modern principle, realize that no tricks, no imitations, no cheapnesses, no pretences of any kind, are tolerable in a Christian church, and that the admission of those things in the temple of the living God is blasphemy. Instead of the cheap and tawdry structures of shingles and clapboards, or flimsy brick and stone veneering, doomed to very desirable decay, we should have once more solid and enduring temples that, even if by reason of our artistic backwardness could not at first compare with the noble work of the Middle Age, would at least take place with it in point of honor instead of standing, as now, a perpetual reminder of our meanness and our hypocrisy.

This is the first and highest reason for church building, and the second is this: the providing of a place apart where may be solemnized the sublime mysteries of the Catholic faith; a temple reared about the altar, and subordinate to it, leading up to it, as to the centre of honor, growing richer and more splendid as it approaches the sanctuary, where is concentrated all the wealth of obedient and loving workmanship that may be obtained by means of personal sacrifice through years that gather into centuries. Previous to the sixteenth century the churches of England were stupendous treasure-houses, in which every jewel and statue and picture, every bit of metal work and carving and embroidery, voiced some personal devotion, some gratitude of man for mercies and blessings. When, at the word of Henry VIII., half the consecrated treasure was torn from the Church and poured into the greedy laps of thieves and sycophants, the spirit of sacrifice and gratitude began to die away; and when at last, at the command of an hypocritical usurper, the last half was dashed into sorrowful ruin by the hands of brutal fanatics, it vanished altogether, and only in these last days is it making its appearance here and there, as the old religious spirit begins slowly to reassert itself.

It is unnecessary to argue for the importance of this exalted quality in church building. Conscience, instinct, impulse, all urge us to glorify, with the extreme of our power, the sanctuary of the Lord. It seems incredible that in the last few centuries this, the eminent reason and law of church building, should have been so grievously obscured, until men should wrong-headedly have reared their auditoriums and show structures, forgetting the supremacy of the sacramental nature of the Church in the zeal for the glorification of her prophetic nature. Such has, however, been the case; but, thanks to recent events, it is no longer necessary to argue for a more just conception of things.

The third aspect of church architecture is this: the creation of spiritual emotion through the ministry of all possible beauty of environment; the using of art to lift men's minds from secular things to spiritual, that their souls may be brought into harmony with God. The agency of art to this end is immeasurable, and until the time of the Reformers this fact was always recognized. Not in the barren and ugly meeting-house of the Puritans, with its whitewashed walls, three-decker pulpit and box pews, were men most easily lifted out of themselves into spiritual communion with God,— not there did they come most clearly to know the charity and sweetness of Christianity and the exalting solemnity of divine worship, but where they were surrounded by the dim shadows of mysterious aisles, where lofty piers of stone softened high overhead into sweeping arches and shadowy vaults, where golden light struck down through storied windows, painted with the benignant faces of saints and angels; where the eye rested at every turn on a painted and carven Bible, manifesting itself through the senses to the imagination; where every wall, every foot of floor, bore its silent memorial to the dead, its thank-offering to God; where was always the faint odor of old incense, the still atmosphere of prayer and praise.

It was the fashion, in a would-be Spartan generation, to scorn all these artistic adjuncts as superstitious and idolatrous;

but the attempt to succeed without their aid was not crowned with great success. Art has been, is, and will be forever the greatest agency for spiritual impression that the Church may claim, despite the ancient and modern iconoclasts. But for its manifestation of supreme art in painting and architecture and ritual, the Church could never have won so quickly the allegiance of the civilized world.

And this for the reason that art is in its highest manifestation the expression of religious things, and that only so, only through the spiritual power of color and form, light and shade, tone and harmony — in a word, through art in all its varied forms — may religion find at once its fullest expression and its most potent incentive. The triumphant architecture, the sublime art, the solemn and splendid ritual that have grown beneath the beneficent influence of Christianity,—nay, that have owed their existence to the Church as surely as they have accompanied her periods of health and vigor,— are the instinctive expressions by men, through the symbolism of art, of the religious emotions she has created. Art is at once the flower and fruit of an age, its glorious manifestation, its guarantee for the future, its fertile seed that needs but to fall in good ground to spring up in tenfold strength. Industrial art depends upon just social conditions for its existence, sensuous art, the art of Athens and Venice, owes its existence to beauty of life and environment; but spiritual and divine art comes only when the religious spirit is dominant and supreme.

That part of the Church which deliberately rejects the ministry of art in her service does so at her own peril,—a peril that history has shown to be grievous, indeed, and inevitable.

If we are to see speedy restoration of Catholic Christianity to universal acceptance, of the Church to final authority, we must abandon our niggardly and parsimonious giving, forsake our flimsy, temporary, chaotic architecture, and build once more churches that, by reason of their massive stability, their richness and their splendor, the voiceful pictures of their walls and windows, the storied stones of their niches and porches and pinnacles, shall not only be worthy of acceptance as the temples of God, but shall show forth to men the mystery and sublimity of the Catholic faith, satisfy their stifled cravings for art and beauty, lift them into the exaltation of spiritual conviction. This is one of the most important aspects of church architecture, as it certainly is the one most recklessly and universally ignored. Only among a people in a land and day when the art instinct has been almost crushed out by evil conditions could this carelessness and indifference maintain. Its origin may be found in certain clearly known historical events, its results may be seen with equal ease.

The fourth aspect of church building is the one which is generally considered exclusively, and is precisely the last in importance of the four that I have named,—the arrangement of a building where a congregation may conveniently listen to the instruction of its spiritual leaders. I do not mean for an instant that this quality must be sacrificed to the others: a church, if it is properly designed, may be a perfect sanctuary, a perfect temple, a perfect auditorium. I only protest against that custom of refusing to consider any plan that shows a single seat behind a column, a nave longer than it is wide, or that does not provide a picture-gallery light during the day and the illumination of a theatre at night.

Some fifteen years ago, when Richardson's death removed the fictitious vitality of the alien style he had tried to make living, and it began to collapse in the follies of "school-house Romanesque," a few architects, working quite independently, began a kind of crusade against the chaos of styles that hitherto

had afflicted church architecture. They began to study the
motives and principles of mediæval Christian architecture
rather than the mouldings. They sympathized with the new
vitality in the Church, and with the movements toward theological as well as historical continuity. They conceived the
idea of giving the Church a form of architectural expression
that should be in conformity with the new tendency. Until the
Reformation the development of architecture in England had
been logical, consistent, healthy. At that time it ceased utterly,
all continuity was broken. From then church architecture had
been entirely artificial and perfectly valueless; and, as the end
of the nineteenth century approached, these qualities had apparently reached the climax of their development in America. In
England the reform had begun with the Pugins, and had been
firmly established by a wonderful line of succeeding architects,
until at last men like Street, Scott, Pearson, Bodley, Garner,
Sedding, Austin, Paley, Stokes, and Wilson, with scores of
younger and equally enthusiastic men, had succeeded in re-es-
tablishing the continuity, and church architecture in England
was a living force again. Upjohn and Renwick had tried to
bring this great movement to America, but its vitality lapsed
with their death; and Richardson had swept the very memory of
it away. The field was clear, and another attempt was made to
do on this continent what the architects had accomplished in
England. The reform was cordially received, it has spread
rapidly, and at last it would almost seem that it had a good
chance of ultimate victory.

In the chapters that will follow this, I shall try to take up
the question of church building from this standpoint,— the standpoint of an architectural restoration,—and show the application
of the ancient and eternal principles to every phase of ecclesiastical architecture, from the country chapel to the cathedral.

# THE COUNTRY CHAPEL

In the introductory chapter I have spoken of the history of church architecture in America, and have roughly named the errors of which we have been guilty, specified the motives, the artistic dogmas, that lie at the root of all good church building. Let us now begin at the beginning, and endeavor to apply these principles, test existing work by them, and see how ecclesiastical architecture will manifest itself at this present day, founded as it must be on the architectural history of all Christian time, with the lesson of the triumphs and failures of two thousand years before our eyes, the nature of our own peculiar civilization, our own epoch always in our minds.

And, above all else, let us remember this: when we build here in America, we are building for *now*, we are manifesting the living Church. It is art, not archæology, that drives us. *From* the past, not *in* the past. We must return for the fire of life to other centuries, since a night intervened between our fathers' time and ours wherein the light was not; and, therefore, it does not come direct to our hand. We must return, but we may not remain. It is the present that demands us,— the immutable Church existing in times of the utmost mutability. We must express the Church that is one through all ages; but also we must express the endless changes of human life, the variation of environment. This is church architecture; the manifestation through new modes of the ecclesiastical past; unchangeableness through variety; the eternal through the never-fixed.

This question will command further and more detailed consideration later on, when we approach the more ambitious work of church building; but it is of great moment here where we

13

are beginning with the simplest of the structures of the Church, the chapel and mission of the country towns. No matter how small they may be, how inexpensive, how simple in design, they are yet churches; and in the least of them one should be able to read as clearly the nature of the power that brought it into existence as in the greatest of cathedrals. The country chapel is a great and unsolved problem so far, at least, as we in America are concerned. Perhaps the building committee does not think it worth while to go to an architect when so little money is to be spent; perhaps some one has fallen upon a " Collection of New and Tasty Designs for Pretty Churches," issued by Western commercial practitioners, and is beguiled by the gorgeous offer of " plans and specifications for one hundred dollars "; perhaps a warden or vestryman knows a deserving young man who is a draughtsman in so and so's office, and will furnish the drawings at half-price. Whatever the cause, the effect is conspicuous; and the country chapel — the kind that costs perhaps from $5,000 to $10,000 and seats from one hundred to two hundred people — is almost without exception horrible in the extreme. Were it frankly rough and barbarous, a frontier log cabin, it would be honorable; but it is not this. It is flimsy in construction and wholly bad in shape and composition; but it is worse than this, for it is made contemptible by its "ornamentation." Even where it is a perfectly square box with a steep "pitch roof," it becomes doubly hideous through the arched windows, the silly wooden buttresses, the futile belfries and pinnacles that are not ecclesiastical, though their creators thought so.

This particular type is no longer to be condemned, for it has passed; and we know it now only from the decaying structures that still-stand, forlorn reminders of our own dark ages and of the mutability of timber. It has passed, but its place

I. EXAMPLE OF FALSE "PICTURESQUE."

II. EXAMPLE OF THE AFFECTEDLY PICTURESQUE.

is taken by a worse and more pernicious style,— that of the chaotic, fantastic, would-be picturesque horror that owes its existence to the deadly shingle, the seductive wood-stain, cheap colored glass, and "the art movement." (See Figures I. and II.)

The commercial "architect," who prints engaging volumes of ready-made plans, is the prophet of this very dreadful dispensation; and it is almost impossible to characterize its wickedness too strongly. The poverty and flimsiness of design and construction struggle to hide themselves beneath a cheap and tawdry elaboration, and the result is both very bad art and very bad morals. Small dimensions are supposed to argue insignificance; and, to counteract this, a diminutive structure is tortured into a grotesque echo of some larger building, with most ignominious result. One constantly finds churches, seating perhaps less than two hundred, where the plan is cruciform, and there are aisles, clerestory, columns of iron or wood; insignificant towers, gables, belfries, and porches complete the already shapeless exterior; and the result is a scandal.

There is just one way to build a country chapel, and that is to build it as simply as possible and of as durable materials as may be obtained. It may turn out to be bald and ugly, but ugliness is better than impudence. A plain and ugly church may be dignified and religious, a "cosey, home-like little place" never can.

This is the problem: to build a shelter for the altar and congregation, together with such adjuncts as are necessary, for the smallest cost consistent with honesty, durability, dignity, and reverence. Let us take the plan first.

In such a church as we are now considering, there could hardly be a vested choir: therefore, the chancel is solely for the altar and clergy. This does not mean that a little recess is enough. More space is necessary than is actually demanded by the function of a sanctuary, for there must be a due proportion between nave and chancel. If we cannot obtain dignity through size, we can through relation: therefore, the chancel should be deep, even if narrow. It need not be divided from the nave by a screen, which properly belongs only in a large church. A chancel parapet of plain panels, with a heavy rood-beam above carrying a crucifix or cross, is the best indication of the transition from nave to sanctuary. Indeed, the choir screen, unless very elaborate, is something of an affectation. It is a question of design. Some churches demand it, the architecture makes it necessary; but more often than not the screen, particularly if it is of metal, is an offence, injuring otherwise good work. Like the transept, it seems to belong in a church of great length and height.

Let the plan of the chancel be as simple as possible. Three steps at the entrance, one at the communion rail, and three to the foot pace of the altar give the right elevation in a church of the size we are considering. The sanctuary should be square, not polygonal. This latter form is dangerous, and but seldom used to good effect, except in cathedrals or churches of great size. In a small church it is inevitably mean and trivial in effect. The lighting of the chancel should be from high windows on one or both sides. In so small a structure a window over the altar, while peculiarly ours by history and tradition, is hardly advisable; for, in order to give the altar its due prominence as the centre and concentration of the church, it should have space behind for gradines and at least a low reredos. In a lofty church there is room for both reredos and windows. In a small church it is difficult to have both without crowding. It is far better to fill the whole end with a dossal reaching to the ceiling than it is to confuse the eye by spots of light and dark, complications of glass, wood, and drapery.

IV.

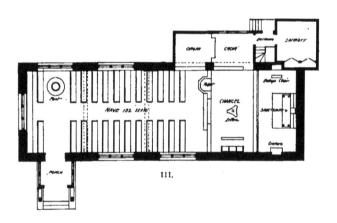

III.

Again, in a short, low church the east window, even if filled
with dark glass, is apt to be dazzling and to attract the eyes
from the altar. Moreover, in a church where there is no choir
in the chancel, it is well to keep this part of the structure quite
dark; for, by so doing, we increase the effect of length and
size, adding as well a touch of that mystery that comes from
shadow,— a quality that should be achieved in every church,
and is easy enough in a large building where one can deal with
aisles, chapels, and lofty roofs. I hope it is hardly necessary to
say that a skylight or any lighting in the roof itself is an out-
rage, and absolutely sure to destroy every particle of architectural effect or religious impression.

The size of the nave is determined by the number of sit-
tings: this, of course; but the question of proportion is a very
different matter. The narrower it is, the better for acoustics,
appearance, and economy of construction. Twenty feet in the
clear is about the minimum; for this gives two pews, each
seating five persons, and a central aisle about four and a half
feet wide. To seat two hundred people, twenty rows of ten
seats each would be necessary, making the nave from rear wall
to chancel parapet about sixty-five feet,— a good proportion.
With every foot the nave is widened and shortened, something
of the effect is lost, while the acoustics are not improved and
the cost is increased. It is easy and inexpensive to roof a span
of twenty feet, but it is three times as costly to roof a span of
double this width.

If it can possibly be managed, the walls should be high, the
roof low in pitch; yet since, where this method is followed, the
walls, to be in good proportion, must be a few feet more in
height than the width of the nave, the quantity of stone in the
walls is doubled, and this means extra cost. On the other
hand, a roof of low pitch costs much less than a steep one; for

you can get a tie beam at the level of the plate in this case, where with a steep roof on low walls you are prohibited from doing this, and are forced to construct an expensive truss. Of course, an iron tie rod is a crime that no intelligent architect would consent to for an instant.

With high side walls it is possible to keep the sills of the windows well above the floor, and this is most desirable. There was once a fashion of making the windows low; but this is a bad plan, and gives extremely ineffective lighting. Where the side walls must, on the score of cost, be reduced in height, the sills of the windows should be kept high, even if the windows themselves become very small. They may not give much light; but this is not a fault, if the west window is made large, for this will sufficiently light the church and from the right point.

The arrangement of the choir space, where the choristers are not vested, is somewhat difficult; but, since this condition is almost inevitable in small churches, it must be solved, and solved rightly. The old-fashioned scheme of organ and mixed choir at the west end in a gallery is good, and is usually followed by Roman churches of whatever size. It is not very popular with us, for some reason or other, probably because chancel choirs have become so fashionable. If it is desired that the music be near the chancel, then a space may be provided opening either into the chancel itself, as in Figures III., VII., and IX., or into the nave, as in Figure V. In either case there should be access to this choir space from outside, so that the singers and organist need not pass through the congregation, and the choir may be shielded from view.

In the matter of design, of architectural style, cost is of course the limiting quality in work of the kind we are now considering; yet economy need not mean inferiority. If the law followed is that of perfect simplicity, it is hard to go far wrong.

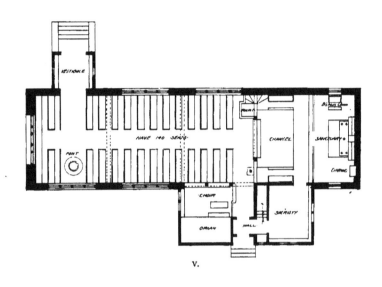

V.

VI.

It is only when there is an ill-considered striving after inexpensive elaboration that there is trouble. There must always be the basis of a long and narrow parallelogram covered with a simple roof, unbroken from end to end. Square plans and complicated roofs kill all repose, all dignity, all effect. A tower is fatal unless it can be large enough to be respectable. The little square erections with or without wooden spires are an offence. As will be shown later, central towers are impossible, unless the church is of good size. The west tower on the axis of the nave, simply a continuation, as it were, of one bay of the nave itself, is the position that is sanctioned by precedent and artistic law; but it is expensive, and almost out of the question in a small church. Figures IV., VI., VIII., and X. show several treatments of the exteriors of small churches, two without towers, one with the western position, one with the tower on the side and used as a kind of chapel or transept. Figure XI. is an example of the chaotic and reckless designing that is an offence to God and man.

We cannot hope to rival the little churches of England in this day and generation, for conditions absolutely prevent the hearty lavishing of labor that was characteristic of the Middle Ages. The cut stone and carving, the elaborate stone tracery, the buttresses and balustrades and pinnacles are out of the question. We cannot restore the externals of the Gothic style; but we *can* endeavor to re-create the underlying spirit, and lead it to express itself in the new forms we must impose on it. We can begin by building in stone, not in wood; for, though it costs more at first, it is permanent, and it is respectful. Almost any local ledge stone will serve if it has a fairly even face: the cobble-stone style, the absurd result of a misguided attempt at the "sweetly-picturesque," is very shocking (see Figure XII.): and it is safe to say that this kind of stone — that is, rounded

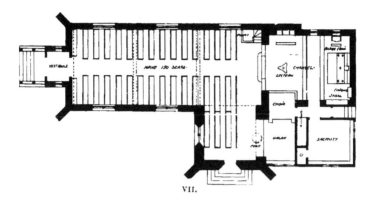

VII.

VIII.

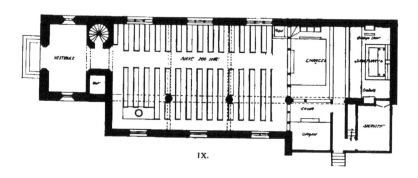

IX.

X.

field stones — can never be used under any circumstance whatever. A wall must have unity and coherency: if it lacks these qualities, it is not a wall; and round stones absolutely prevent these results. What is called "seam-faced" granite is the very best material where it can be obtained. In the Central West, limestone and sandstone are comparatively cheap; and they, of course, make an ideal wall, provided they are used with a sawed or dressed surface. The so-called "rock-faced" ashlar is exactly the wickedest building material, next to round field stones, that has ever been used. Where stone is out of the question, brick may be employed, if it is common red brick with a rough surface and is laid up in common mortar. Fancy brick and colored mortar can *never* be used.

In the matter of interior treatment the law of simplicity and reserve holds equally good. Stone, except in the smallest quantities, is out of the question because of its cost: brick has yet to be used successfully in this country; plain plaster finish for the walls seems the only alternative, and, when treated in flat color without the slightest attempt at decoration, is dignified and respectable. The roof must, of course, be wholly of wood. The barbarous mode of half a century ago of filling in the panels between the trusses with plaster is out of the question, and probably no longer suggests itself. The construction of the roof should be of the simplest; and, if oak or elm is too expensive for the sheathing, cypress can be used. Indeed, in the simplest churches, the framing may be of the ordinary building timber, planed, of course, and in any case, whether natural oak or spruce, stained dark brown and finished with a dull surface. American woods in their natural condition, with the exception of black cypress, which is most beautiful, but very expensive, are too yellow and too light ever to be employed. This is particularly true of hard pine, which is bad in color and does not take stain well.

XI. EXAMPLE OF VICIOUS DESIGN.

XII. EXAMPLE OF BAD STONE WORK AND AFFECTED DESIGN.

The question of stained glass will be taken up later. Here it is only necessary to say that, unless figure windows by the best men can be had, it is better to use plain "cathedral glass" in some warm color, set in diamond-shaped quarries in heavy leads, than it is to try to get an effect with cheap glass.

All the richness and cost in the furniture should be lavished on the altar, which may be made as elaborate as the money will allow. It does no harm to have an altar of immense richness in the plainest little church; but an elaborate pulpit and lectern, particularly if they are of lacquered brass, are in exceedingly bad taste, if they outshine the altar. Of course, they are pretty sure to be in bad taste, anyway, if they are in brass,—a material that can only be used very sparingly. Even in very small churches the altar should be large, eight feet in length being about the minimum, though side altars may be shorter. The bishop's chair, which is a throne only in cathedrals, should be very simple, and should stand to the north of the altar and facing it. The credence is placed on the south, as are also the sedilia for the priests, should these be necessary. The communion rail should always be very simple, fancy brass work being most out of place. Where there is no vested choir, the lectern may very well stand in the centre of the chancel, before the altar, in the old monastic fashion. The best form is the carved support with a triangular, revolving book-rest. The pulpit should be on the north, or gospel side: it should be well elevated; and, the plainer it is, the better. As I have said above, the trade pulpit of lacquered brass is exceedingly wicked. One thing that it is well to remember, particularly in small churches, is that the lighting at night should be from the side, not from central chandeliers, since these are dazzling, and conflict with the altar.

Sometimes there is not money available even for a church

of the roughest stone, and wood is the only material that can be used. Where this is the case, it is better to treat the new building as a frankly temporary shelter, built to last only until a real church can be erected. It is foolish to waste a dollar on such a structure as this, and it is better to spend no more than what will barely suffice to make a shelter than to throw it away

XIII. EXAMPLE OF GOOD ENGLISH DESIGN.

on boards and shingles. One can worship God in a barn; but it is denied to us to build flimsy wooden shanties to His glory, and to try to deceive Him by the cheap ornament wherewith we hoodwink our neighbors. If it is worth while building a church, it is worth building it well; and, if this generation has not the funds, then let the work wait for the next.

Wood is a fascinating material, particularly in the form of shingles: one can build much with it, and at small cost; but the temptation to frivolity and fantastic complication is almost irresistible. It is easy to pile up irregular gables and porches and belfries, and the result is popularly held to be picturesque; but it isn't, it is only silly. Great or small, a church must have dignity and reserve; and where great size does not give these things, in spite of the vagaries of the unhampered architect, it is particularly necessary that the utmost care should be

XIV.

exercised to get the proportions right and the first effect simple and even severe. Recently a fashion has developed of treating a small church like a cottage, of trying to obtain an effect of "cosiness," which is quite the most wrong-headed scheme that has offered. A church is a church, not a sitting room; and, even if it seats only a hundred people, it must be a church in every detail. Consider the old English churches shown in Figures XIV. and XVI. They are very small, yet they are unmistakably religious in their function; while figures I., II.,

29

and XI. might be school-houses almost, or libraries, or fire-engine houses. They are without self-respect, without nobility, even without decency.

XV. EXAMPLE OF GOOD ENGLISH DESIGN.

The little parish church of England is the most perfect type ever produced, and must therefore be for us a model in every way. The fad for "Romanesque" is dead, fortunately; and the latest fashion, "Parisian Renaissance," can never be applied to church work. We have tried many things, but, in the end, we are driven back where, logically and historically, we belong; and, if we try to do what our English forefathers did, without trying to copy their work, we cannot go very far wrong.

In Figures III., IV., V., VI., VII., VIII., IX., and X. are shown plans and exteriors of small churches studied from this source. They are not copies of English originals: they are only inspired by them. It would be possible, of course, to measure some old church and reproduce it exactly; but this

XVI. THE PERFECT TYPE.

would be inexcusable affectation, it would be bad art. Into every design produced at this time must enter something of the personality of the architect, a great deal of the contemporary quality of the church. Our sense of economy forbids our making a church any larger than is absolutely necessary; and so we cannot have the dark aisles with their stone piers and chiselled arches, the side chapels and chantries, the lofty roofs and deep chancels that are such facile means of producing structures of dignity and grandeur, so sure a guarantee of mystery and awe in the final effect. Neither do we altogether need these adjuncts to nave and chancel as yet. Therefore, we must do the best we can without; and, though the task is harder, it is not beyond the powers of our achievement. With study and seriousness of purpose, we can build small churches that shall be as religious and as worthy in their degree as the cathedral itself; and this is an absolute duty.

Reduced to a sentence, then, is not this the law of church building as applied to country chapels? Build in stone or brick; plan with rigid simplicity; design both exterior and interior with reserve, formality, and self-control; have the mass simple, the composition equally so; imitate no form or detail of larger structures, but work for the dignity and the reverence that are theirs; above all, let the spirit be that of the unchanging Church, the form alone that of the present day.

# THE VILLAGE CHURCH

It was in England during the Middle Ages that this particular type of religious architecture — indeed, of the religious life it so beautifully expressed — reached the highest point of its development. On the Continent the cathedral seemed the unit, the ecclesiastical centre of the people of a region; but in England, where the village was more perfectly developed, the parish church became the vital centre of a community. In this land, which is also our own, it is not so much the cathedrals that inspire our wonder and admiration as it is the matchless little churches, scattered so lavishly over a fertile land that even now, after revolution and brutal iconoclasm have done their worst, scarcely a village is to be found where there is not at least one church redolent of the love and self-sacrifice and devotion of perished generations.

There is a strange personality about these churches, an intimate, human quality that one looks elsewhere for in vain. They are without splendor or magnificence; they possess nothing of the premeditated grandeur, the proud magniloquence, of the cathedrals and abbeys; there is little evidence of a clear and preconceived design. They are simply the living monuments of the sane and healthy devotion, of the joyful Christian faith, of men to whom religion was the beginning and end of all things, — even though there was much between.

The village church was the centre of civilization; it was the source of education, the guardian of the privileges of the people, the spring of material aid and spiritual consolation. In all healthy society there is an inextinguishable hunger for beauty, and this hunger the Church satisfied in the fullest degree. Set in an environment of natural beauty, the enduring stone was

33

raised in fabrics that, if not imposing and awful, were always grateful and satisfying. All over the exterior the stone masons, not then unthinking mechanics at so many dollars a day, wrought out their fancies, their ideals, even their merry humors, through the stubborn but enduring medium of sandstone and

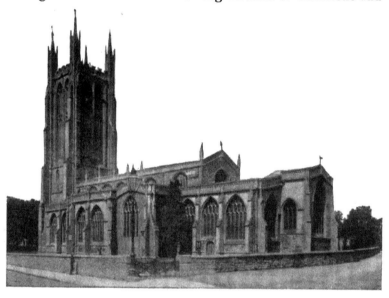

XVII. ST. CUTHBERT'S, WELLS.

marble. Within, every man and woman capable of crafty handiwork — and this then meant the whole body of the people — found a fair and welcoming field. Great windows rich with fantastic tracery were to be filled with splendid glass; the altars were to be adorned with fretted screens and canopied niches and carven figures of saints; stalls and pulpit, lectern and sedilia were to be reared of fine woods and chiselled into marvellous

richness of panels and pinnacles, canopies and poppy-heads. There was an organ to be built and cased in elaborate wood-work, lamps and candlesticks to be wrought of yellow brass,

XVIII. CHURCH AT HARBERTON.

and sacred vessels of gold and silver, studded with precious stones. There was leather to be gilded and embossed for seats and wall hangings and the covers of missals and breviaries, and the latter themselves to be engrossed and illuminated on vellum and parchment. There were frescos and religious pictures to be painted, damask and tapestry to be wrought, altar vestments,

35

Austin & Paley, Architects.

XIX.   ST. GEORGE'S, STOCKPORT.

copes, stoles, and chasubles to be embroidered. Finally, there were the memorial brasses to be graved when, one by one, they became necessary, and, perhaps, the altar-tombs, the chantries, and the chapels.

So the parish church grew like a living thing; and, as it developed, it drew to itself every soul in the community, tying them by every bond of love and memory and association. It was never completed; for it was living, and finality was impossible. It was not only the symbol of human unity: it was that unity, made up of all that lay within its control.

An inexhaustible field for the loving labor and the pious industry of the people, it became as well the source of delight and æsthetic satisfaction for new generations. Picture galleries and museums and concert halls were unnecessary; for here was all art freely given, and in its highest forms. A constant incentive to artistic effort, the parish church became the very power that made this effort possible, inspiring men, educating them, creating in them the impulse to art work, giving them the very ability to make it possible.

There came a day when, in the providence of God, a nation gone mad was permitted to shatter the lace-like carving into ragged fragments, to beat the delicate statues into ruin, to cart the jewelled windows away and dump them into ditches, to burn the fretted woodwork and the precious vestments and the illuminated missals, and to hand over to a few crafty knaves the jewels and the treasures that had been consecrated to God.

Whether or no this episode may be looked upon as a sufficient cause, it is quite clear that the description given above does not apply with accuracy to the modern parish church in American villages. Of course, the conditions have quite changed; but, if we cannot have now a village church that shall be the church of the whole people, we ought at least to have

one that for those who worship there should be something of
what similar churches were a few hundred years ago. Of course
where a church is open only at the hours of service on Sunday,

XX. ST. JOHN'S, COVENTRY.

this is quite impossible; and the building must remain a purely
artificial fabric, without personality or sympathy. There is a
very popular movement to reform this altogether; and, though
it started in the larger cities, it is extending rapidly into the
villages. To be sure, one might criticise it in certain ways, par-

38

ticularly on the score of its apparent devotion to the development of the parish house to the total disregard of the church; but, in spite of errors, the tendency is wholesome and righteous,

XXI. CHURCH OF OUR SAVIOUR, MIDDLEBOROUGH, MASS.

and when, by and by, it extends from the parish parlor, the kindergarten, and the bowling-alley to the sanctuary, it will have found its true bearings, and begin to show the noble results that will then be possible.

But even now there is no valid reason why we should not

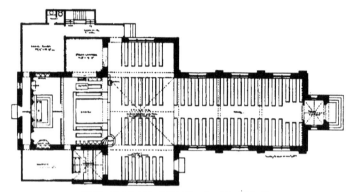

XXII. PLAN OF CHURCH OF OUR SAVIOUR.

XXIII. CHURCH OF OUR SAVIOUR, MIDDLEBOROUGH, MASS.

accept the old idea of the church as a fabric, and, recognizing the very unique and exalted nature of the problem, and the honorable results that are possible, try to build village churches that shall be worthy to stand with those our forefathers built in the old home four centuries ago. We *don't* do it: we build recklessly, thoughtlessly, extravagantly, often; and, as a result, our village churches are no more consistent than are our secular buildings. Who is to blame? Well, every one connected with the work, in some degree. The rector, perhaps, because he has been in England and has read "Parker's Glossary," and so thinks that he can lay down the general lines of the design and direct the chosen architect; the building committee, because they have certain practical theories which they insist shall be expressed or followed; the congregation, because they will make no sacrifice in order that the new church shall be as beautiful as those in the Middle Ages; the architect, because he has not the slightest sympathy with ecclesiastical architecture, doesn't know what the word "Gothic" means, and is interested only in getting a conspicuous edifice and his commission. Above all, the chief blame is to be attributed to the nature of the times in which we live, when impatience demands a completed structure on the day of dedication; when everything must be done by hired workmen, perfectly indifferent and without any feeling for beauty; when the "Ecclesiastical Art Furnisher" is rampant, and public opinion does not make it a crime to buy his wares. We have been so long without art that it is no longer instinctive, but is become a commodity that the building committee expects to buy from its architects.

Verily, it would seem that there *were* reasons why we should not build as our fathers builded in the fifteenth century; but, if so, there are none why we should not *try* to do so. It is being done every day in England: why not here? Not that we

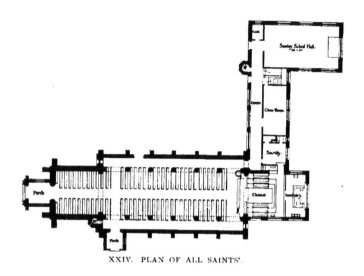

XXIV. PLAN OF ALL SAINTS'.

XXV. ALL SAINTS', DORCHESTER (BOSTON).

should wholly succeed: this must be forever impossible, or, at all events, out of the question until we have a civilization that once more makes the appreciation of beauty and the ability to do artistic work instinctively, as much a part of life as it was then. But we could at least have the honor of trying, and the results would be better than those that confront us now.

To build a church rightly, it is necessary to do three things: first, to build in the only style that we have any right to, and that has any kinship with the American branch of the Anglican communion of the Catholic Church; second, to select an architect who believes in the Church and sympathizes with her, who understands Gothic as a living, not an historic style, and then to rely on him implicitly; third, to build a little now, and build it right, instead of trying to build a great deal, and as a result building it meanly. Let us consider these three points.

The matter of style is vital: there is a vicious tendency to follow a fashion, and so obtain something "up to date" in design. This is quite fatal. There is one style, and only one, that we have a right to; and that is Gothic as it was when all art was destroyed at the time of the Reformation. But this is only the basis: from this starting-point we must advance, in order to prevent a dead archaism. We can't work in some perfected period of Gothic, like Early English, for example, or Decorated, or Flamboyant. Neither can we use Norman or Romanesque, and still less can we wander into the delectable but pernicious paths of the Renaissance. This would be affectation; but we *can* assume anything we like from these styles or from any others, so long as we assimilate them, make them integral parts of a great whole. But the base of it all, the primary architectural impulse, must be that of the last days of Gothic architecture in England; namely, the end of the fifteenth century.

XXVI. ST. ANDREW'S, DETROIT, MICHIGAN.

XXVII. ST. MARY'S, HERTS.

It is hardly necessary to prove that Gothic is the one style in which we can work. This is generally admitted, now that the late architectural episode has died in the humiliation of "school-house Romanesque"; and the new fashion of Parisian Renaissance has nothing to offer, and so *per force* drives its devotées to a cynical disregard of the Church. But "Gothic" as a term has not as yet differentiated itself. Too often it means anything done in any country of Europe between the thirteenth and sixteenth centuries. Hence we only have buildings that try to appear, in detail at least, of some particular time and some special land. This is archæology, not architecture. If we are to build honorably, we must take up the life of church building where it was severed, and continue from that point, adding what we will, of course, so long as we assimilate it, borrowing anything that is available from earlier periods, even from as far back as the Norman. But the root must be the English Perpendicular Gothic of the early sixteenth century.

Doing just this is what has made the English church architects of this generation great men, and has created a vital school of church building in that country. Doing just the reverse is what has abandoned us to chaos.

The selection of an architect is quite as important a matter as the restriction of style. It is apt to be left almost to chance. There are scores of really great architects in America. There are, perhaps, a half-dozen who feel Gothic, understand it, and can therefore work in it as the Church must demand they should work. There are many who can copy Magdalen tower intelligently, who can draw accurate thirteenth-century mouldings, and who can select good tracery from photographs and measured drawings; but these are not available men if we are to build *living* churches. Yet, if a church is to be built, a competition is announced; and any architect who has a friend at court is asked to submit designs. He may be an "archæol-ogist," a classicist, a patron of Romanesque; but it is assumed that at least he can design so simple a thing as a Gothic church. Then, when the plans are all in, the building committee, half

Bodley & Garner, Architects.

XXVIII.  HOARCROSS CHURCH.

of whom have perhaps never been in England, pick out the scheme that looks best on paper, regardless of the abilities or the sympathies of the designer.

Then the authorities begin their instructions. "There shall be no east window, for we don't like the light in that place." "No: we can have no big columns to obstruct the

XXIX. ST. STEPHEN'S, COHASSET, MASS.

McKim, Mead & White, Architects

XXX. ST. PETER'S CHURCH, MORRISTOWN, N. J.

view of the pulpit." "Those windows are too high: we must have the sills lower." "A $30,000 church without a transept and a polygonal chancel and a fine steep roof? Absurd! We must have all these things." "A rose window is very lovely: put one in the front. And we must have a triforium and a narthex and a cunning little octagonal baptistery, by all means."

XXXI. EXAMPLE OF UNINTELLIGENT DESIGN.

This is hardly the way to build a good church. In the first place, a competition is exactly the worst way to choose an architect. Instead, one should be selected solely on the ground of the work he has done; and, once chosen, his hands should be free until the day the church is consecrated. In only one thing should he be held under rigid control, and that is the matter of cost. In design, materials, methods, his word should be final.

I grant that it is quite wrong that this should be so. We

ought to be able to build a church without the intervention of an architect, but we can't. He is a product of the new conditions of life wherein art is an exotic, no longer the inalienable right of the people ; and, so long as these conditions continue, he is a necessary evil. No single architect can build as perfectly as the old priests and abbots and stone masons ; but he can build better than anybody else in this day and generation, and so he must be accepted and his authority recognized.

I have said above that, in order to build well, it is necessary to build a little and build it right. Let us suppose that a village parish has $30,000 to spend on a church to seat three hundred people. The tendency nowadays is to try to get a structure complete down to the last electric light burner and square foot of carpet. To do this, everything must be " scamped." The walls must be of rubble, plastered inside ; the cut stone of the exterior, perfectly plain, without moulding or carving ; the window tracery must be of wood, and the floor also ; the chancel furniture, thin and plain ; the whole design, small, unimposing, and poor. Twenty years later the structure is outgrown and shabby. Then it is torn down ; and the $30,000 is lost, or else twice the sum is expended in unavailing attempts to magnify an insignificant thing into dignity.

The money spent on such a building, if devoted to the construction of just so much of a great design as was necessary to provide for the religious offices and the accommodation of the people, would not have been wasted. A lofty choir might have been built, together with, perhaps, half the nave. All the stone for future carving might have been put in place, but left rough. The tower and porches might easily have been left until some future time. Reredos and choir screen, carved stalls and statues, could all have been temporarily omitted, and the church, bare and awkward, if you like, would yet have been permanent and honorable, and right as far as it went. There would have been an incentive to further effort on the part of the congregation; there would have been the certainty that the structure was permanent, and so men would be encouraged to add some bit of carving, some statue, some window; above all,

Austin & Paley, Architects.

XXXII.  ST. HELEN'S, LANCASHIRE.

there would be a building with history and with constantly growing associations. It would have been a living thing, a monument growing and developing from year to year, becoming ever more glorious and more beautiful.

Granted the true, historic, and living style, and an architect with ability to work seriously therein, the result would still be inadequate and even wrong if the church were not designed

50

after this fashion, as a thing that should grow from year to year, never quite perfect, never finished.

In using the word "village" to describe the particular kind of church that we are now considering, I may have conveyed an erroneous impression. The word was used rather in the English sense than in the American, and the churches referred to are such as would be built in what, in this country, we call small cities; that is, those under a hundred thousand population. Between churches of this kind and those that would be built in a large and crowded city there is a distinct difference. In the former instance a more spacious site is easily available. The houses are not built in blocks, and are not apt to crowd up around the church, as in large cities. Moreover, a certain formality, elaboration, and refinement of detail are desirable in large city churches; while in those we are now considering there may be something of greater simplicity.

Let us consider one or two practical points. In plan the church must be long and narrow, not only on account of acoustics, but for emotional and artistic effect as well. In the case of a village church, much greater height is necessary than in a country chapel; for the low church with spreading roofs is admirable only in rude country districts. The walls of the nave should never be less than the width between the columns, and should indeed be a little more. The choir and sanctuary must be deep, if possible twice their width. The sanctuary cannot be less than twelve feet from east wall to communion rail, where the foot-pace of the altar is raised three steps above the sacrarium floor. The depth of the choir is dependent on the number of choristers. In addition to the length required by the choir stalls, ten feet is necessary to provide for the alleys at either end of the stalls, the kneeling space in front of the communion rail, and the three steps to this level from the choir pavement. Each row of stalls should be raised a step at least above the one in front. The chances are that in any church of this size provision for a vested choir must be made, and very likely for an auxiliary choir of women as well. Where the latter is necessary, by far the most dignified and ecclesiastical

XXXIII. STRATFORD CHURCH.

method is to provide a kind of "nuns' gallery" on one side of the choir and looking down into it. This is perfectly satisfactory from a musical standpoint. It gives a chance for a fine architectural effect, and it also solves the vexed question of the manner of vesting female choristers.

The plan of the body of the church will almost inevitably be the old fashion of a central nave, long, narrow, and high, with low and still narrower aisles on either side.  As I have said before, the cruciform plan demands a central tower, since it is impossible to treat open, intersecting roofs in any good architectural fashion.  Such a tower is very expensive, and so it is usually out of the question.  Where the church is cruciform without aisles, the cost is not very great; but this scheme is not a very safe one in so small a building.  It is apt to diminish the effect of size both outwardly and inwardly.  The three-aisled plan is by far the best, and may even be considered the classical type.  It may be varied almost infinitely.  The aisles may be wide and low and filled with pews, or they may be high and narrow and used only as ambulatories.  This latter mode gives a certain formality and stateliness that seem more consonant with the city church than with the type we are considering.  In All Saints', Dorchester (Figures XXIV. and XXV.), the aisles are narrow and low, the clerestory being very high and containing the chief range of windows, those in the ambulatories being very small and filled with dark glass.  Where there is an insuperable prejudice against seats behind columns, this scheme can be followed; for it gives the requisite shadow behind the arcades and yet leaves all the seats in the open.

This prejudice against columns that cut off a direct view of the altar or pulpit from a few seats in the side aisles does not seem to be one which is based on reason.  Not only does the omission of these arcades of columns and arches militate very seriously against the dignity and impressiveness of a church interior, it also is almost certain, particularly in the case of large churches, to destroy all sense of just proportion.  Where great length is obtainable and the number of seats is not excessive, accommodation may be provided within the lines of the columns, as in the case of All Saints', Dorchester; but it is almost impossible to increase the width of the central

XXXIV. CHURCH AT SONNING.

XXXV. CHURCH AT CHILHAM, KENT.

nave beyond the limit of thirty-five feet without enormously increasing the cost of the church or else quite destroying the effect of proportion. Where a long nave is not possible and five hundred seats or more are required, there is no way of providing for this except by placing them in side aisles. Of course, this results, as I have said before, in cutting off direct view of the altar from a few seats; but this is by no means fatal. There are plenty of seats, with a direct view, in the nave itself; and those in the aisles which have not this are few in number. The prejudice is rapidly dying out. It is an heritage from Puritan times, and one which is not destined to endure. A little reasoning will show that it is absurd to sacrifice every question of dignity and proportion for the sake of what is in reality only a prejudice.

Not only are side chapels almost indispensable conveniences in churches of any size, they are also the source of most beautiful effects of light and shade, and give the "opening out" effect at the east end of the church that is so desirable. One chapel is usually all that is necessary in village churches; and this should be in the most accessible portion, with an independent entrance or else opening out of the side porch. Oftentimes this side chapel can be so arranged that in winter it can be shut off from the church by traceried screens filled in with glass. This makes it possible, on occasion, to heat the chapel alone, which is sometimes a distinct convenience; yet, when the full seating capacity of the church is demanded, the screens can be opened or moved back. Usually it is well to have the morning chapel on the same side as the sacristy, in order that both the high altar and the side altar may be served from the same place. In the "typical plan" that I have shown, the chapel is arranged after this system. This is a particularly good place for a memorial tomb, if there should be demand for such.

There are, of course, a great number of technical points that I might refer to in connection with the details of an ideal church: the size and contours of the piers with their spacing; the nature of the arches (that is, whether they should be two, three, or four centred, and whether they should be sharp and pointed or wide and low); the size of the windows; the

XXXVI. PARISH CHURCH. WATERLOO.   Paley & Austin, Architects.

design of tracery,—indeed, all the many points that must be carefully considered by any conscientious architect. These are, however, as I have said, technical considerations; and, since the object of this essay is not to lay down rules whereby any architect or layman may design a church to suit himself, but rather to indicate the general principles which govern church building, it is unnecessary to refer to this here.

The things most carefully to be avoided in planning are precisely those that are modern innovations. Not because modern fashions cannot be good, but because in church architecture they do not happen to be so. The mediæval builders worked at their problems just as did the Greeks; and, like them, they succeeded in finding exactly the right way to do things. But they had what the Greeks had not, and that was the inspiration of Christianity. Therefore, the style they created was far more mobile, personal, variable. It gave an almost unbounded field to the imagination, it permitted infinite variety in detail; but back of all this liberty were the fundamental laws of proportion and of composition. When we began to return to Gothic as the one ecclesiastical style, we quite ignored these essentials, and tried to amuse ourselves with details alone. Hence the errors that have been made, and that persist vigorously even now.

One of the worst of these errors is the stubby, cruciform plan without columns and with low side walls, a steep roof supported on heavy trusses, and a polygonal chancel. On these lines good or even tolerable results are absolutely impossible. An architect who would follow them is just as criminal as one who would change the proportions of a Greek temple. This unpardonable corruption owes its existence in a large measure to the persistence of the old Puritan meeting-house prejudice against columns or piers or any architectural feature that would differentiate the structure from a lecture hall. The fancied necessity of getting rid of all obstacles to direct vision, together with the very absurd theory that a square plan rather than a long one gives the best acoustics, is responsible for the shapeless and ignorant edifice that has usurped the place of the really Gothic, Christian, and Catholic church.

What, then, is the scheme of a typical village church? To

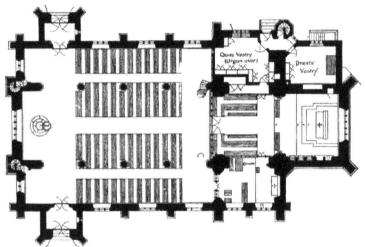

XXXVII. PLAN OF ST. MARY'S CHURCH.

Micklethwaite & Clarke, Architects.

XXXVIII. ST. MARY'S, STRETTON-CUM-WETMORE.

me it seems something like this: The main lines are those laid down by centuries of precedent. At the west end is the tower and main entrance; the body of the church is laid out on the simplest lines; a nave 24 to 27 feet wide and 75 to 90 feet long is separated from the aisles 13 to 15 feet wide by arcades of arches supported on stone shafts 15 feet on centres. For its architectural effect the body of the church depends on perfect simplicity, on the shadow in the roofs, and on the play of light and shade from the large windows in the aisles and the small ones in the clerestory, and the many shafts with their curving arches. As one approaches the chancel, however, the building begins to expand and reveal effects of distance, of width, of profound shadow and sudden lights. The main lines of the nave, of course, continue straight to the altar, broken only by the chancel arch and the screen or rood beam ; but outside these main lines, that seem to give strength and simplicity, all is variety and elaboration. On the north the aisle opens out into the deeper shadow of the baptistery; on the south the morning chapel affords the requisite distance; yet the aisles themselves narrow on either side of the choir into low and comparatively dark ambulatories, that give through the arches of the choir, half filled with traceried screens, the shadow necessary to emphasize the brightness of the choir and sanctuary.

A good Gothic church must begin in simplicity at the western entrance and then develop in two ways simultaneously as it reaches the choir: it must draw in, concentrate, until it converges on the high altar; and it must open out, expand, reveal vistas into chapels, ambulatories, aisles. It is hard to describe just what is meant, and it is impossible to explain why it should be necessary, why it should be an essential part of the Gothic idea; but it is, as witness almost all churches of the Middle Ages, and for a contrast those so numerous ones of modern times where the principles are forgotten, and hard walls and no vistas whatever make erudition worse than useless. Westminster Abbey is a good example of the ideal type, or must have been so until it was turned into an exhibition of inferior mortuary sculpture. St. Mark's in Venice, though not Gothic at all, is quite as good an illustration. Trinity church in Boston will

Paley & Austin, Architects.

XXXIX. ST. MARY'S, DALTON-IN-FURNESS.

serve to show what is the result of abandoning a firmly established law.

In the "Typical Plan" the object is to obtain the utmost richness of effect, of varying light and shade, of space and distance, of ultimate mystery, if you like, without unnecessary expense. I do not mean by this phrase that there should be any parsimoniousness, any meanness in building, but that there should be neither wasteful size nor unnecessary adjuncts. It is such a church as should be built by a parish of perhaps two hundred communicants. To build it rightly and all at once would cost, of course, a very large sum; but to build the chancel, sacristies, and four bays of the nave, leaving out all the carving and ornamentation for a time, and letting the rest of the nave, the tower, chapel, and baptistery, remain for future years, would cost no more than is spent on many churches of equal accommodation, but finished with tower and everything else complete. Of course, in such a church as this, floor and walls should be of dressed stone. Stone vaulting is practically out of the question, except for towers, porches, and small chapels. To vault a nave with stone means not only immense cost, but an elaborate system of flying buttresses; and these are too ambitious for anything except cathedrals or very large city churches. I need hardly say that vaults of lath and plaster, or of steel construction, are utterly and forever impossible to an honest architect or a God-fearing congregation. The vault is not an essential part of Gothic architecture, though pedants and archæologists have said so. A fine roof of simple open beams supported on carved stone corbels is infinitely better for such a church as we are considering than a stone vault, even were this possible from a financial standpoint.

In designing a village church, the architect has a problem before him that admits of no rival: the opportunity is incomparable. In the country chapel the limitations of cost prevent any richness or elaboration or the working out of any good ideas. In the city church the limitations of land are equally hampering, though in a different way. The village church conceived as a monument to endure for ages and to develop year by year, the cost being limited only for the moment, becomes almost the noblest problem that offers. It stands midway between the country chapel, verging in its design and materials on roughness, and the city church, with its necessary formality and stateliness. Absolutely simple in conception, it must be reserved and powerful in its composition, classical in its proportions. But, these qualities once attained, it may blossom into almost unrestricted richness of detail and ornamentation. The popular modern church that tries to be effective through a multiplicity of parts is merely foolish, though the church is free to cover itself with splendor as with a garment.

For the materials of the exterior, while there is a little more license than in the case of city churches, there is less than in the country chapel. "Field" or "quarry" stone, if it has an even surface and good color, can be used; and "seam-faced" granite is always good, not only because of the surface, but for its extraordinary beautiful color. "Rock-faced" sandstone, "cobble-stones," boulders, or split granite, are out of the question. For very formal and refined work, dressed sandstone or limestone is necessary; and these materials should always be used for carved work and trimmings. Brick,— red brick, that is,— with plenty of stone worked in for quoins, string courses, and trimmings, is used admirably in England, but badly in this country, though there is no possible reason why this latter condition should exist. Whether brick can be used successfully for interior work is still a question. For roofing, copper is about the only good covering: slate is too hard and cold, while tiles are out of keeping, and many kinds are of very doubtful durability.

A matter of the utmost moment in the case of village churches is that of their surroundings. Too often questions of temporary or fancied convenience mar what might otherwise be a most noble structure. It should not be forgotten that the village church is in a way a more vital part of the life of the people than a city church. It should afford them the blessings of art and beauty that otherwise in our peculiar civilization may be quite absent from their lives. Not only should the church itself be without and within a combination of all pos-

XL. TYPICAL PLAN.

sible beautiful things, it should also, from its very location and surroundings, be a constant inspiration. Land is not fabulously valuable in villages, and there should be enough of this. The ideal scheme is that of a great and beautiful church in its own churchyard, surrounded by the tombs and graves of its own people; but, even if this is impossible, there should at least be ample land with trees and shady paths, so that the church may stand withdrawn a little from the streets and the secular life around. For the meeting-houses of the denominations that are used once or at most twice during the week, this is not necessary; but for a church that should be a part of the daily life of its people it is most important.

It cannot be too constantly held in mind, it cannot be too steadily reiterated, that a village church is in its nature a matter of paramount importance, not only from an architectural standpoint, but from that of civilization. It is not the Sunday club of a certain organization: it is, or should be, the concentration of the life of the people, the greatest influence that is brought to bear upon them. As it was in the past, so it should be now. The village church should be the spiritual, ethical, and artistic inspiration of the people. If it fails in any of these directions, it is inadequate. If it succeeds in all of them, then it is triumphant. Let us, then, make our village churches what they once were centuries ago,— monuments of the devotion of the people, and, as well, a supreme agency satisfying all their infinite desires for beauty of every kind.

It is not necessary to study very carefully the ancient English churches I have used to illustrate this and the preceding chapter, to see how perfectly they fulfil this requirement. A single glance at St. Cuthbert's, Wells (Figure XVII.), Harberton (Figure XVIII.), St. Mary's, Herts (Figure XXVII.), St. John's, Coventry, Stratford, Sonning, and Chilham (Figures

XX., XXXIII., XXXIV., and XXXV.), will show how intimately they are of the people, how redolent of the soil, how
deeply religious, yet how personal, simple, and, as it were, irresistible. Those that built them loved every stone that came
consecrated to God from under their hands. They are as
much a part of England as her trees, her birds, her denizens of
the moor and forest, her people. These are but one or two of
an innumerable list, and each is a lasting memorial of nameless
yet honored dead. Consider the little church at Chilham.
It lies in the midst of its green wolds as unconscious of its perfect beauty as were the masons who reared its walls; yet in every
line it is almost faultless, and it shows forth not alone the right
instinct for beauty that marked the men of the Middle Ages,
and that is the rightful heritage of all men, but also the
simple, honest, manly reverence and devotion that are an equal
heritage. Contrast this of ten thousand others equally good
with Figures I., II., XI., and XXXI. of ten thousand others
equally bad, and then say, if you can, that we are erecting just
monuments of a civilization that we loudly protest is at least
equal with that of the past.

Bad as these new churches are, we are not without some
consolation in the shape of work, mostly as yet in England,
that is not unworthy to stand with that of the fifteenth century. In Hoarcross and Stockport (Figures XIX. and
XXVIII.) and in nearly all the work of those English architects I have named in the introductory chapter, we find both
the old impulse and the old results. Hoarcross and Stockport
are crystalline in their delicate perfection. Study them carefully, and you shall see what constitutes right church building.
In each of them, as seems to be inevitable in all contemporary
work, there is something of self-consciousness, of the striving
for perfection; but attribute no blame for this to the architects.

The cause lies in the spirit of the epoch, and no one man shall escape it.

And, if we fail of the ancient naïveté and unconsciousness, as for a time we must, we have yet, as in those two churches, a certain unity, a certain "passion for perfection" that has the most noble results; and for this we must be grateful forever.

# THE CITY CHURCH

If in what I have called the village church ecclesiastical architecture finds its opportunity for the highest expression,— short of the cathedral, its highest, since it is less modified and hampered by circumstance,— certainly in the city church it

XLI. ALL SAINTS', BROOKLINE, MASS.

obtains its fullest chance of showing its adaptability to conditions essentially modern and almost without precedent. It is here that Christian architecture is privileged to prove its extreme adaptability, its vitality, its power of fitting itself to new conditions without losing any of its historic and spiritual qualities.

In the great periods of church building in the past the city was but an exaggerated village, so far as its physical aspect was concerned. The streets were irregular and winding, land was not cursed with the incubus of an artificial valuation, the houses and shops were low, varied in style, and not sequent

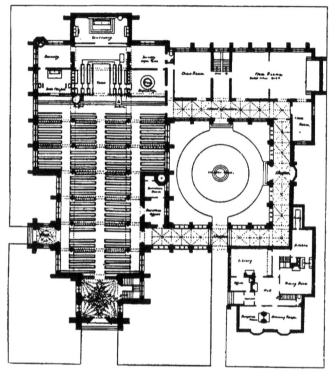

XLII. ALL SAINTS', BROOKLINE, MASS.

in unbroken blocks, trees and gardens and orchards broke the monotony of buildings, and in every way extent was about the only quality that differentiated the city from the village.

As a result, the churches of a city, particularly in England, differed in no radical particular from the churches of the country. Indeed, many of them were but suburban foundations overtaken and surrounded by the marching town; and, however much they might be rebuilt and restored, the primal characteristic remained, and the church still stood in its ample yard, low, gentle, and reserved, yet sufficiently dominant in an architectural way. Now, of course, all this is changed. The modern city is a thing unheard of before; and with its straight, uninteresting streets, its towering structures, its dull blocks of houses and shops, demands quite other methods of design where religious edifices are concerned.

Yet how persistently the greater number of architects refuse to recognize this, and continue dully to design churches that might perhaps be acceptable in towns and villages, but become insignificant and without architectural value in a great city! Well designed they may be in themselves, but this is not all of architecture. A building, to be good, must not be puffed up with insolent individualism: it must recognize the fact that it is only a part of a great whole, and that it has duties in addition to those it owes itself. It must adapt itself to new conditions, conform in a measure to its environment, and, if the latter is unprecedented, so must it be also. Yet this is almost unrecognized by the majority of architects; and, as a consequence, we find churches with low walls, many little features, slender spires, and all the other accessories of country design, set down in the immediate proximity of blocks of dwellings or mercantile buildings that lift absurdly above them, crushing them into ignominy, making towers that do not rise above the neighboring cornices grotesque and laughable.

But in England, whence come all right impulses in the revived architecture of Christianity, this blunder has been noted; and already the line of reform has been indicated. I have illustrated several of the notable designs, and shall refer to

XLIII. IN THE CLOISTER, ALL SAINTS'.

them later. In the mean time let us consider the architecture of city churches apart from this most important question of adaptability to environment.

Of course, in all fundamental particulars church building in the city is identical with church building in the country. The same laws as to style hold good, the same principles of planning and composition. The necessary modifications are only such as would be suggested by the now necessary economy of space, by compulsory concentration. In certain respects detail and design must be modified ; for the city church, with the cathedral, is the culmination of the development in richness and refinement from the beginning in the country chapel. Here any suspicion of rudeness is out of the question, picturesque effects are futile : the material must be refined and delicate, rough stone is barred and in its place must come stone that has a smooth and well-dressed surface, or brick, if it is used properly. Ornamentation must be finely cut and carefully placed : everything must be refined, reserved, even formal. It also seems right that the last vestige of domesticity,— if I may call it so,— of homeliness, if you like, should be done away with, that the church may take on the qualities of power, formality, even of grandeur, that fit it for its new position. The design appropriate for a grove-shaded cottage in the open country would be monstrous on a metropolitan boulevard, and the same is true of a church. Cottage or palace, the home is still there ; and, hillside sanctuary or looming minster, it is still the church of God. In each case adaptation to conditions has been necessary only.

It is true that in a city there must be two kinds of church building, that for the outskirts where land still has something of its intrinsic value and where as yet the surrounding buildings are comparatively low and scattered, where the streets are wide and there are good trees, and that for the already crowded sections where land in quantity is not available and where blocks perhaps eighty or a hundred feet high strive to crush every non-commercial structure in their vicinity ; but in the former instance the logical design is simply that of the village church, refined and elaborated in material and design, as

I have said, and conceived with a view to the almost inevitable future, when tall buildings will try to annihilate its dignity and effect. In the second instance, where a church must be built in a busy quarter on land of great value, a new set of conditions

XLIV.

must be confronted. In Figures XLI., XLII., and XLIII., I have shown the plan and two exterior views of a church now being erected under the more conventional conditions. Sufficient land is available, and the surrounding houses are low and inoffensive blocks of dwellings. For many years the church must dominate the whole section, yet ultimately it must find itself in juxtaposition to lofty structures. Therefore, since it is to stand

74

for centuries, it must provide against this contingency. Hence it is very lofty in its main walls, which rise some sixty feet

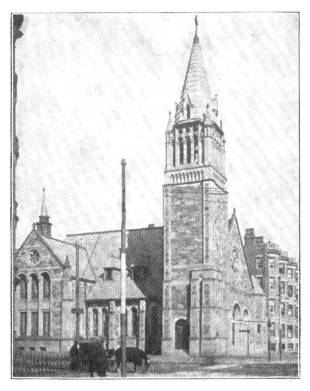

XLV. A CHURCH DWARFED BY ITS SURROUNDINGS.

above the street; and its tower lifts to the imposing height of one hundred and seventy-five feet. Its masses are all simple, its parts few. It is calculated by its very simplicity to hold its own against all comers. The plan is one that offers a solution of the vexed question of seats in aisles; at the west end, where such seats would, by reason of the size of the columns, be almost wholly cut off from any view of the chancel, the aisles are only narrow ambulatories, which, nevertheless, give the requisite variety and shadow, while near the chancel they

Henry Vaughn, Architect.
XLVI. CHRIST CHURCH, NEW HAVEN, CONN.

widen out into chapels, almost every seat in which has a view of the altar. This arrangement obviates the necessity of genuine transepts, which, as I have said before, are not very successful in any church lacking the proportions of a cathedral.

The arrangement of the parish building and rectory around a cloister is a scheme the virtue of which will be apparent

76

when the whole section is solidly built up: then the green and quiet court-yard, with its traceried cloisters, and its gabled roofs and mullioned oriels lifting above, will be very grateful and a soothing relief from the dull and dusty street. In Figure XLVI. is shown another church worked out on lines that are absolutely right. There is the loftiness of the walls and the perfect simplicity of parts that must always mark any city church that is conceived with due regard to its environment. Moreover, it has that singular refinement, that courtly self-respect, that seem indispensable. It could not be taken for a country church; yet it is pure and scholarly Gothic, both modern in feeling and mediæval,— the enduring style adapted to new conditions.

Figures XLIV. and XLV. are examples of city churches that have been designed with scant reference to their surroundings, and therefore fail completely. I do not refer to the merits of their respective designs, but only to their adaptability to environment. Both are insignificant, and some day will seem more so, just because they were designed as if they were to stand in open country. Notice the crushed and apologetic air they both display, with their low side walls, their roof ridges, and even their towers, hardly rising to the level of the cornices of the surrounding blocks. There is no evident reason why this modern trick of cottage walls — bad even at the best — should have been adopted. Due regard for the unities of architecture would have prompted lofty walls and powerful masses. Instead we have quite the reverse.

Let us now turn to the other category of city churches, that of the buildings that must from the beginning stand in the midst of surroundings that do their best to be dominant. Where solid blocks crowd on every side, it is nothing but folly to hold by the precedents of the past. The church must be the chief structure in the group; and, architecturally, it must command its neighbors. To do this, its walls must rise to the highest possible elevation: I mean the walls of the nave itself.

Leonard Stokes, Architect.
XLVII. NEW CHURCH, MANCHESTER, ENG.

It does no good to build a low church, and then try to lift it into dominance by means of a towering spire. The result of this course is failure. The nave, the main body of the church, is what tells; and this must lift itself into supremacy, even if this is at the expense of a tower. For, after all, this latter feature is not an essential. A church may be just as good without it.

XLVIII. NEW CHURCH, MANCHESTER, ENG.

Take, for example, Figures XLVII., XLIX., and LII. They show designs calculated for their locations, lofty, massive, commanding. The amenities of Gothic are done away with, and stress is laid on its attributes of power and domination. The Manchester church is a particularly good example

of the way in which a church may be so designed as to secure
its unquestioned architectural supremacy and yet be good

XLIX. ST. S EPHEN'S CHURCH, FALL RIVER, MASS.

Gothic.   In the interior, again, one feels the essential bigness
of the design and of the designer.   Every inch of ground
space is made available;  yet there is adequate  variety, shadow,
composition.    It is a perfect type of city church.

In its great simplicity it is also a model.  That a church should
become as rich and splendid as possible is true ; but oftentimes

this is taken to justify what can only be called tawdriness, not only of decoration, but of design. There is a certain school of

L. CHURCH OF THE ASCENSION (R. C.), NEW YORK CITY.

ecclesiastical art decoration rife just at present that, not content with overlaying plain surfaces with the most gaudy and meretricious ornament, strives to torture the very architectural forms themselves into quite meaningless elaboration. Now there is no limit to the richness that is desirable, if it is honest and real, if it is in the shape of goldsmith's work and sculpture and

81

LI. CHURCH OF ST. MARY THE VIRGIN, NEW YORK CITY.

wood-carving and tapestry and good stained glass, not in the form of gold leaf and lacquered brass, *papier-maché* and opalescent glass; but this richness must be backed up by fine, solid, and simple architecture. The finer and franker the lines, the more reserved and powerful the parts, the greater the richness of the decoration that may be allowed. No amount of splendor could make this church at Manchester weak or effeminate.

In this noble building one finds also the spaciousness, the largeness of proportion, that are so essential in city churches. By the very nature of things the ritual is more varied and elaborate than in the village church; and it is imperative that the chancels, and particularly the sanctuaries, should be very large. The little huddled niches that still linger among us are relics of a crude period and deserve to be done away with. Breadth, depth, a wide space between the fronts of the choir stalls, another between the stalls and the communion rail, and yet another between the rail and the lowest of the altar steps,— these things are most necessary for the conducting of a dignified service, and one that shall not be huddled and confused.

And this spaciousness, this largeness of design, applies as well to all other portions of the church,— to the piers and arches of the arcades, the side chapels and other accessories, to the windows, the doors,— indeed, to every portion of the interior. And the same is true of the external design. The church that is confused by many turrets and gables, porches, irregular roofs, and varied towers, is not only bad in itself, but less effective in urban surroundings than would be the case, were its masses bold, simple, and powerful. There is a good deal of real Greek feeling in an old Gothic church; and beneath all its richness of detail and splendor of sculptured ornament there is a great, solid foundation mass that is instinct with power and command.

It is this that tells in the case of a church designed to stand in a great city, and only such a church is able to assume its just position of supremacy.

The church illustrated in Figure LI. was conceived in the right spirit. It was given the height and the simplicity of mass that were necessary; but most unfortunately it was built after an

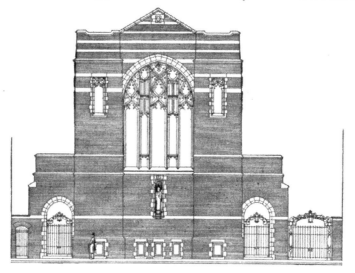

LII. A MISSION CHURCH.

evil fashion, falsely and unpardonably, with a frame of steel like an office building, supporting the sheathing stone that was worked into the forms of honest construction. It is therefore an example of all that should be avoided, when it might quite well have been a marvel of ecclesiastical beauty and holiness, had it but been a piece of self-respecting and honorable construction.

I have spoken of this point before, the prime necessity of

rigid honesty in church-building, where any wilful falsity approaches the point of sacrilege; but it cannot be dwelt upon too strenuously in this age of expedients. False construction is simply a lie told for reasons of penury or ostentation.

There has been altogether too much of this sort of thing of late. Imitation stone and mosaic, make-believe chimes, imitation marble, and even stained glass, all the tricks of trade are quite bad enough in civil and domestic affairs; but, when they enter into the question of church-building and ornamentation, they become unpardonable.

We may study the monuments of tne great past until we are surfeited with erudition. We may measure and sketch and photograph the work of the Middle Ages until we could almost reconstruct any given monument. We may try to build with archæological exactness, and in this we may succeed; but we may as well understand at once that, until we realize that beauty of whatever kind in any church is put there to the glory of God and not to the admiration of the passers-by, we may study and labor in vain.

If a church is not honest,— honest in its design, its construction, its decoration,— it is nothing; and any added richness, if it is the richness of falsity, is only an added shame.

And not only must a church be honorable in its construction, it must also be good in design. This sounds like a truism, but it is not; for, when they are carefully considered, it will be easily seen that the vast majority of contemporary churches are exactly the reverse. I do not speak now of the question of style, which I shall consider when we come to the supreme glory of religious architecture, the cathedral, but of essential rightness in whatever fashion may be chosen. For there is a right and a wrong in every style, and the wrong is without excuse so long as there are those who can do the right. Consider

LIII. TRINITY CHURCH, NEW YORK CITY.

for a moment Figure L. Now it would not be fair to say that the wrong is always of the violent type exhibited here, but it often approaches it ; and, after all, when a thing is once bad, it matters little what degree of badness it may have achieved. The question of right and wrong is not a matter of taste. The fact that the majority of a building committee or the reputation of a given architect testifies to the excellence of his designs has nothing whatever to do with the case. There are certain fundamental laws of planning, composition, proportion, construction, and design, that are as old as the art of architecture itself: they are to be found equally in the Greek temple, the Byzantine basilica, the Gothic cathedral. These laws *are*, and by them architecture must be tested. If it falls short, it is without excuse. If, like Figure L., it violates every one of these laws, and if in addition — and again like Figure L.— it is without a glimmer of vitality, of nationality, then it is an insult to God. For it is not enough that the construction should be honest and of the best. It is necessary that the art that makes the thing living should be of the best also. " The best " — that is inadequate enough ; but it is the least we can give to the glory of God and the honor of the Church, and, if we fail of this, then we fail, indeed.

Good architecture, perfect art, are not matters of pride : they are not desirable because they flatter the feelings of a certain congregation, but because they show a right impelling spirit, because they are indeed " the outward and visible sign of an inward and spiritual grace " in that congregation, and because in their perfection they are the least unworthy of the material treasures of this life that may be offered in the worship of God.

# THE CHANCEL AND ITS FITTINGS

We have now considered the church in its various estates, from the country chapel, through the village church to that of the modern city. Before passing to the crowning fabric of Christian civilization, the cathedral, let us take up a little more in detail certain elements that go to the making of a typical church, such, for example, as the chancel and its furniture, the altar and its various appointments in the shape of vestments and sacred vessels, stained glass and decoration, and the other details that must in themselves be right if the church is to be worthy of its ancestry and of its object; and, first of all, let us consider the sanctuary and chancel, both in point of arrangement and in regard to the different fittings that must be provided, leaving the chief object, the excuse and reason for the church itself,— the altar,— for a special chapter.

I need hardly say that the chancel and sanctuary are not only the most sacred portions of a building consecrated to the service of God, but also almost *the* church, the nave being but an adjunct of more or less size provided for the shelter and the convenience of worshippers. The altar is the nucleus, the heart of the whole matter, the sanctuary the space provided for the priests who minister at the altar, the chancel the shelter of those "ministers," whether clergy or choristers, who aid in surrounding the altar service with due solemnity and splendor, the nave the area set apart for those for whom the service is offered. Thus there is a steady progression in sanctity from the porch to the altar-stone, and this progression should be expressed in the fabric and the enrichment of the church. The

nave may, as I have said, be plain and formal, variety is not desirable and lavish decoration out of place, but with the choir

I.V. CHANCEL OF ALL SAINTS', DORCHESTER, MASS.

screen there is a change; and both from the standpoint of reverence and from that of artistic composition it is imperative
that, to borrow a musical term, the crescendo that culminates
in the climax of the altar itself should begin here.

90

Cope & Stewardson, Architects.

LIV.  CHOIR SCREEN, ST. LUKE'S, GERMANTOWN, PENN.

It is not necessary that there should be an arch separating the chancel from the nave, it is not even necessary that there should be a choir screen,— either or both of these features are good if properly used: it is simply a question of design, and here the architect's word should be the deciding power. Where a church is long, narrow, and high, an arch gives a noble effect, and the same is true of the rood- or choir-screen. In many cases, however, a low parapet with a big rood-beam above, as in Figure LV., is better than the screen. Where the latter feature is used, it may be made extraordinarily beautiful, as in Figure LIV., which is from a church in Germantown and is one of the best pieces of ecclesiastical wood-carving in America. It should, however, always be of wood. At least this should be so unless we can learn from some of the old screens in Spain how to use metal for this purpose. As matters stand now, the trade screen of brass or iron is abhorrent and hardly to be endured.

The rood-beam, particularly if it supports a carven Calvary or a painted icon of the Crucifixion, is capable of being made singularly effective ; and it is altogether too little used. In certain old churches this beam became a rood-loft, often of amazing richness; but it is hard to see any particular justification for this feature now, and its charm is often that of its antiquity alone. In Figure LVI. both loft and beam are used with fine effect. Figure LVII. is a fine example of the best type of rood-screen, though for some unaccountable reason the Corpus is lacking from the cross. Figure LVIII. shows a splendid old loft from which the Calvary has been removed.

Of the furniture connected with the chancel, yet generally just outside its limits, the pulpit, lectern, and litany desk are the most important. What I have said of the screen is true in a large measure both of the pulpit and lectern ; that is, that they are best if made of wood. Not that metal is out of the ques-

LVI. ST. AGNES'S, KENNINGTON, LONDON.

tion.   In ancient times it was well employed, and stone also; but nowadays the temptation of lacquered brass is too much for us, and the results are unfortunate.   If anywhere there should be solidity and a certain grave dignity in a pulpit; and, where this structure is wrought of filigree brass or iron, the effect is fatal. The same is true in a large degree of the lectern.   There is no possible reason why it should be in the form of an eagle; and there is every reason why, if an eagle is used, it should be as conventional as possible.   The realistic bird with natural feathers is, of course, bad art.   In Figure LIX. I have shown a very beautiful eagle lectern of modern English make, and in Figure LX. another design, wrought out on older lines.   The triangular lecterns, such as we find all over Europe, are not only convenient, but uniquely beautiful; and we can only hope that their use may be restored.

When the pulpit stands on the Gospel side of the church, as should always be the case, the lectern is usually placed in a corresponding position on the Epistle side; but a usage that is now being restored is the placing of the lectern in the middle of the space between the rows of choir stalls and directly in front of the altar, though it is, of course, much lower, since it stands on the lowest choir level.   In many ways this position is more convenient and dignified than any other.

Viewed solely from the standpoint of the architect, the lectern is, next to the altar itself, the best subject for design that the Church offers; and, now that the curious mania for eagle lecterns is dying away, there is a chance to make these beautiful objects what their general lines and the requisites of their function make possible: there is no limit to the conceivable variations of design and material.

The litany desk has acquired a certain novel importance of late that hardly seems reasonable.   As it is used only now and

LVII. CHOIR SCREEN, NEWCASTLE CATHEDRAL.

then, it should be brought out only when needed, instead of standing, as sometimes happens, a stumbling-block at the head of the centre aisle in season and out of season. The nature of its service demands, of course, the plainest and most austere design. Indeed, a simple faldstool is about the best thing that can be used.

Entering the chancel, let us now consider its general disposition. First of all, let me argue for space, for generosity of treatment. Crowding is quite out of the question. Here we must have ample room : even if the church is small, the chancel must be big and dignified. (See Figure LXI.) There must be ample space between the front rows of choir stalls,—eight feet at the very least, and as much more as possible. Except in very large churches the nave and choir cannot be over twenty-eight or, at the most, thirty-two feet wide between piers ; and, where three rows of stalls on each side are necessary, this only leaves from ten to fourteen feet for the open space. Where length is possible, it is better to have only two rows of stalls on each side ; for, the deeper the chancel, the better it is in every way.

Each row of stalls should be lifted one or two steps above the row in front, these steps being carried across the choir beyond the seats. The rear row of stalls should, if possible, be divided into separate seats and covered by traceried canopies, those nearest the choir parapet on each side being distinguished from the others by greater richness of treatment. Where there are three rows of stalls to a side, the rear rows are properly clergy stalls, the two at the west being, of course, for the rector and curate.

Picturesque and alluring to the architect as is the old scheme of returned stalls,—that is, stalls facing the altar against the screen,—there seems scant justification for the

mode, except perhaps in cathedrals, so it is hardly to be com-
mended.

For the decorative treatment of clergy and choir stalls there
is no lack of good models in England and on the Continent.
In the canopies of the former, cost is the only limit of richness.

LVIII. SCREEN AT BRODNINCH, DEVON.

Fretted and wrought into intricate design of leafage and tracery,
they may become lasting memorials of faithful and loving
craftsmanship, and every detail of enrichment adds to their
value as an evidence of devotion,— at least, this should be so,
for it was in the wonderful past; but nowadays, when craftsmanship has yielded to trade, it is hard to find the artist in
carving who puts *himself* into his work with love for his labor
and for the object of that labor. Still, such men exist, fortu-

nately; and their work is priceless in its value. I am glad to write the name of one of them,— I. Kirchmeyer, who carved the "poppy heads" of the stalls shown in Figure LXII., each one of which terminates in a little figure hardly six inches high, of the various ministers of the church, from the acolyte, thurifer and chorister to the deacon, priest, and bishop.

Beyond the choir seats there will be at least three steps to the kneeling space in front of the communion rail. Where space and funds permit, there may well be more. In a large church, the higher the altar is raised above the floor of the church, the more visible and dignified it will be. Five steps give a good elevation. Then, with one at the communion rail and three to the foot pace of the altar, you will have about the least elevation that will be dignified and well proportioned.

The communion rail is likely to be a difficult question. Fortunately, the old days, when lacquered brass, wrought iron, and even cut glass and encaustic tiles were considered fit materials, has passed away; but still the rail is likely to remain a rail or balustrade still, and this is seldom dignified. Perhaps the best form is that of a *prie-dieu*, a movable kneeling-bench with sloping top and richly wrought ends. This may be either open or solid, and may include gates that may be closed after the entrance into the sanctuary of the priests and acolytes.

After the altar and reredos the important features of the sanctuary are the sedilia for the bishop and the priests, and the credence. The bishop's chair is always on the Gospel side: the sedilia for the priests are on the Epistle side, where is also the credence. A bishop has his throne only in his own cathedral. In a parish church, while it is right that there should be special sedilia for the bishop and his attendant chaplain and cross-bearer, or acolytes, it is, nevertheless, well to bear in mind that this is in no sense a throne, and should not be treated as such. Yet it should be distinguished by the episcopal insignia of the mitre, the crossed keys, the crosier, etc., and, where possible, should be covered by a canopy of rich carving. The sedile should be divided in three, either by a chair and

LIX. A MODERN ENGLISH LECTERN.

two flanking-stools placed in a canopied recess, or, like the priests' sedilia, by arms and vertical screens. A faldstool or kneeling-bench is placed in front of the bishop only. (See Figure LXIII.) The priests' sedile is also divided in three, for the priest, deacon, and sub-deacon. It should be similar to that of the bishop, but less elaborate; and it is always desirable that the seats should stop some four inches short of the wall to allow space for vestments. (See Figure LXIV.)

The credence should be sufficiently large to take all the altar vessels, cruets, etc., and also the two candles, if this should happen to be the usage of the church. It is decidedly more

LX. LECTERN IN ALL SAINTS', DORCHESTER, MASS.

convenient on the south wall of the sanctuary than on the east wall; but, as the former is also the location of the priests' sedilia, it is often hard to obtain a sufficient depth to allow of this, and perforce the east wall is chosen. As good an architectural treatment as there is, is that of the canopied niche, the lines

being similar to those of the sedilia. (See Figure LXV.)
Where it is possible to carry the lines of the reredos around

J. D. Sedding, Architect.
LXI.  HOLY TRINITY CHURCH, LONDON.

on either side, including the credence, bishop's and priests'
sedilia, and connecting with the organ case and canopied
stalls, the whole being tied together in front by the rood-
screen, the effect is both rich and reserved, full of dignity and

architectural quality. Where this is done, the windows come of course above the line of woodwork, the cresting of the latter reaching just to the window-sills.

In the decoration of the chancel there is the widest range

LXII. CHOIR STALLS, MIDDLEBOROUGH, MASS.

of possibilities. Carved and traceried stone with little statues in their fretted niches, richly wrought woodwork, stamped and gilded leather, tapestries, wall paintings,— if they are good,— all may be used to create a composition of the utmost richness. When to this are added the light from painted windows, the flicker of burnished brass in the shape of candlesticks and hanging lamps, and, above all, the crowning glory of the altar and reredos, an architectural composition is obtained that is unique in its potentialities.

Yet the chance for solemn effects is often most recklessly thrown away. I do not need to describe the commoner sort of chancel: we all know it, with its lacquered brass and futile carving, its cheap tile-work and cheaper frescoing. For this sort of thing architects and decorators are more to blame than any others. The desire for the right thing exists, but too often only to be betrayed. As church architecture is precisely the noblest form of the art and the one least to be mastered by any system of contemporary instruction, so it is the one least studied and least considered. Architects and decorators and " Ecclesiastical Art Furnishers " offer their wares with serene self-satisfaction, quite ignorant of their own ignorance, and potent to play upon the credulity of church authorities who desire only what is good. Until a few years ago there were in this country only one or two architects who could really design a true church, and no men whatever who could furnish good decoration, whether in the shape of glass, metal work, carving or embroidery. This condition has changed, but, unfortunately, the inadequate men still continue to offer their services and their products; and church authorities, naturally ignorant of the merits of various men and the things they produce, are lured into accepting bad art when really they want only what is good. Fortunately, the Church has largely escaped the blandishments of those quacks who print showy books of (happily) impossible structures, the alleged "architects" who are unknown in the profession and who inflict strange horrors on the unwary denominations; but it is a question if the more august corporations and the more eminent architects who possess intelligence that is misdirected, and compel popular

LXIII. BISHOP'S SEDILIA, ALL SAINTS', DORCHESTER.

admiration through the gorgeousness of their products, are not really more dangerous. Blatant ignorance deceives only the ignorant, but a great name and glittering splendor may easily deceive the very elect.

After all, there is but one test,— the test of what has been;

LXIV. PRIESTS' SEDILIA, ALL SAINTS', DORCHESTER.

and this must always be applied to modern church work, in order that we may know if it is good.

In Figures LXVI. and LXVII., I have shown plans of chancels arranged in accordance with precedent and the demands of convenience. In All Saints' the dimensions, particularly of the sanctuary, are somewhat restricted; but nowadays this is likely to be almost unavoidable. Some day we shall realize that the choir and sanctuary do not fulfil all their requirements if they are just large enough to pass — and no more; that the nave must be the first consideration, the chancel but an adjunct. The choir I refer to was not built after this fashion,

LXV. CREDENCE, ALL SAINTS' CHURCH, DORCHESTER.

but rather with a perfectly clear idea of its primacy. Still, it could well have been made a little deeper, and would have been so, had the architects realized the importance of the church they were building. Figure LXVII. is the typical or, rather,

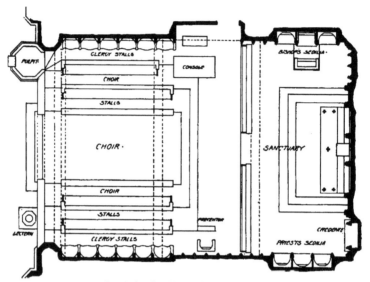

LXVI. CHANCEL OF ALL SAINTS', DORCHESTER, MASS.

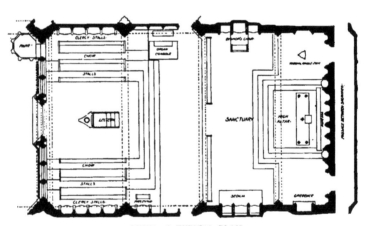

LXVII. A TYPICAL PLAN.

ideal chancel, with plenty of space, adequate elevation, and ample sanctuary. This is the type to which all chancels should approach as nearly as the conditions will permit.

When it was held that one priest in the service of the altar was all that could be required, the cramped old chancels were adequate perhaps from the standpoint of economy and practicability; but, now that the altar service is almost universally surrounded with the dignity and solemnity established as the reverent usage by centuries of Christian life, these no longer serve, and a shallow niche is barred forever, in its place coming the wide and spacious chancel, the many sequent steps, and the sanctuary, where ample room is provided for a grave and solemn ritual.

# CHAPELS, BAPTISTERIES, AND SACRISTIES

Closely connected with the church proper, and forming a part of its fabric, aiding also in making up the total of the dominant idea, are the various features to a consideration of which this chapter is devoted. A church is not solely the altar in its sanctuary, with the choir or presbytery adjoining, and beyond the shelter for the congregation of worshippers. It is the whole wonderful composition and combination of parts that together make up what is really the most perfect architectural fabric thus far evolved by man. In the baptistery we find the porch of the temple of God, through which all men must pass. In the chapels we find the outward sign of the honoring of certain of the saints, not for themselves, but for the showing of God in them. In ancient times we had also the record of the piety and devotion of men who showed in this wise their gratitude for mercies and blessings. In the sacristies we have rooms which in themselves are not secular apartments, but tinged with the sanctity of the sanctuary,— a fact too often carelessly overlooked. All of these integral parts of the church must receive study and consideration equal to that given to the church itself. Let us consider them one by one.

It is difficult to reconcile one's self to the process of change that has reduced the baptistery, once a thing of honor and dignity, a structure that showed through its very solemnity and importance the greatness of the sacrament to which it was consecrated, to an insignificant font hidden in an aisle, crowded against the wall, or, in violation of all right sentiment and just teaching, intruded into the very chancel itself. Surely, the baptistery should possess that architectural importance that its functions argue, and so give to the font the eminence it de-

Sir Robert Lorimer, Architect.
LXVIII. FONT, COCKINGTON CHURCH, DEVON.

mands. Formerly the baptistery was a building apart, second in importance only to the church; and its lesson was clearly read. Where this cannot be now, we can at least isolate the font in its own area, and so design its architectural surroundings as to give it its due eminence.

W. R. Lethaby, Architect.

LXIX. NEW FONT AND CANOPY, BENTHAM CHURCH, YORKSHIRE.

As I have said before, the ancient position of the baptistery was either before the church or at its very entrance, so symbolizing its function as the point of the beginning of the Christian life. The symbol is precious, but it is not of supreme value. Convenience and modern usage may seem to demand a position nearer the chancel, and there is no good reason why this should not obtain. In Figure LXX. it is shown on one side of the choir, the morning chapel being in a corresponding position

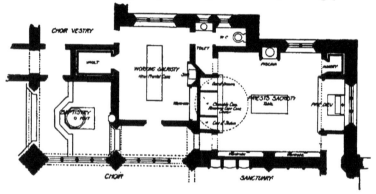

LXX. ARRANGEMENT OF BAPTISTERY AND SACRISTIES.

on the other side; and this is a very convenient position, near the sacristies, and easy of access from the parish building. The font is so placed as to give it prominence and dignity. Behind may very well be a niche with a statue of Saint John the Baptist. In Figure LXXVI. it forms part of the side chapel. This, also, is a good position, both from a practical and an architectural standpoint.

The font, like the altar, should be of stone; for this is solid and everlasting. In shape it may vary widely, and also in size, though it should always bear a certain relation to the size of the church. The drain must, of course, communicate directly

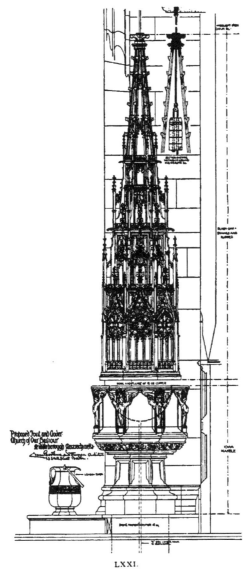

Proposed Font and Cover
Church of Our Saviour
Middleborough Massachusetts

LXXI.

with the earth, never, under any circumstances, with the system of sewerage. A cover is imperative; and this must always be fixed firmly in place, except when the font is in use. I have seen fonts filled with flowers upon occasion, and there should be no opportunity for this unconscious irreverence. In the design of the font cover there is an opportunity for almost unlimited richness. Where this cover can be suspended from the roof and raised and lowered by counterweights, perhaps the best results may be obtained. In Figures LXVIII., LXIX., and LXXI. are shown various types of fonts, with their covers. Figure LXXI. is of the traditional type, an elaborate, spire-like fabric rising to a great height. Figure LXIX. is slightly varied from old modes, and is a good example of the vital and original design that characterizes the new school of industrial art in England. Figure LXVIII. is still more original: too much so, perhaps, since it has a certain suggestion of the old well-curb.

As I have said before, baptisteries and chapels are of the utmost service architecturally in breaking up the contours, in developing the shadows, in gaining the effect of mystery that is so necessary to any good architectural scheme; and it is quite wrong to disregard them. Of course, their chief justification is essentially religious; but in addition to this is the architectural reason, and this we cannot afford to ignore. A good church from an artistic standpoint is composed of sanctuary, choir, and nave of the utmost simplicity of design, gravity of massing, refinement of proportion, classicism of composition, and, beyond this, of bounding walls, following varied lines, giving space, distance, variety, mystery. The central portion must be full of a clear, diffused light, dying away in shadow above; but beyond the nave arcades should be infinite variety of light and color, and this we obtain by the use of baptisteries, chapels, and aisles.

Hardly any church is built nowadays that has not at least one chapel; and, from an architectural standpoint, the more there are of these, the better. In Figure LXXII. I have shown the plan of a very perfect little English church, where the ar-

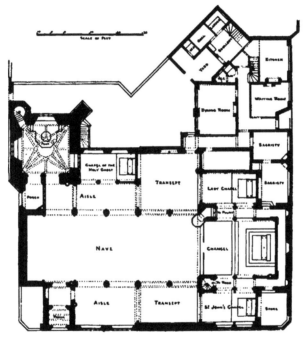

LXXII. CHURCH OF THE HOLY ROOD, WATFORD, HERTS.

rangement of chapels, and of the baptistery as well, is about as perfect as may be. These chapels are so arranged that, wherever one may look, one sees little altars subordinate, but all leading up to the high altar itself.

Where there is only one chapel, it will be used largely for daily services, therefore it should be easy of access. The size is, of course, dependent on the particular needs of the parish; but it should be so placed that all the seats may be available when the service is at the high altar. In the transitional period between the barren days when the church was securely locked from Sunday night until Sunday morning, and the present time, when it is usually open daily from sunrise until sunset, the chapel that could be shut off from the rest of the church, thus effecting an economy in the heating, was temporarily useful; but this consideration seems to have passed. At all events, it is passing rapidly; and so it is seldom necessary to provide a chapel that may be isolated upon occasion. When it is demanded, curtains are usually sufficient. Sliding or rolling doors, nine times out of ten, are an offence and destructive of all religious feeling.

Of course, the sanctuary of a chapel need be of no great size; and the altar also will bear its due proportion to the chapel itself. The credence should be as near the altar as possible, since the priest may frequently be without a server. For the same reason, many steps to the foot-pace are undesirable and unnecessary. Two stalls only are requisite, one on either side of the chancel. If possible, they should be outside the communion rail, as should the lectern as well.

Of course, the small size of a chapel makes possible much finer detail in the ornamentation, much greater richness and elaboration; but everything must be subordinated to the whole church, forming a part of its unity. The same is true of its exterior. One of the most delightful qualities of the mediæval churches is the frankness with which rich little chapels are built on wherever they are wanted, differing in scale and detail from the original fabric, yet harmonizing perfectly in the final effect. (See Figure LXXV.)

If the cobbler should stick to his last, so should the architect

LXXIII. LADY CHAPEL, ST. MARTIN'S, MARPLE.

be careful not to go beyond the limits of his own province; but he may surely express the hope that, for the sake of the art he follows, there may be a return to the clustering chapels that go so far toward giving a church richness of composition and splendor of effect. In the dedications there is a great opportunity for individuality; and, as a result, each church takes on a certain personality that differentiates it without separation.

In Figure LXXVI. I have shown such a chapel as would be appropriate for daily services where only one altar is required in addition to the high altar. The baptistery is arranged in connection with it, and forms the westernmost bay. As will be noticed, it is conveniently placed with reference to the side porch, and may be entirely separated from the chapel or used in connection with it.

One mistake that is frequently made in the building of churches is that of failing to provide adequate sacristy accommodations. Even in large churches we frequently find only a priest's sacristy and a choir vestry. This is quite inadequate. A working sacristy is imperative. The priest's sacristy should be neither an anteroom nor a study: it is for the vesting of the clergy, and for this only. The choir vestry should be used as such alone. An altar — or working — sacristy is absolutely necessary. This is the room for the altar guild, if there is one, and for the acolytes, if the usage of the church calls for them. It is also for the sacristan. Indeed, it is a kind of central office of administration; and without it a church is seriously hampered. Here the flowers are prepared for the altar, the altar vestments stored and made ready for use, altar ornaments cleaned and taken care of. This room may also be used for vestry meetings and by the wardens. A large chest or case in the centre will hold frontals and superfrontals. There should be a sink and tables for the preparing of flowers, cases or racks for banners

LXXIV. NEW ALTAR, ST. MARY'S, CHADDESDEN, DERBY.

and processional crosses, storage for candles and incense,— if they are used,— presses for the vestments of the acolytes, a brazier for kindling charcoal, a large safe or vault for the storing of the more valuable ornaments, the books of the parish, etc.; indeed, provision for the thousand and one things that go toward making up the modern service in its richest form. If possible, the working sacristy should be located between the priest's and the choir sacristy, and it should be so placed as to give immediate access to the chancel. In Figure LXX. I have shown a convenient grouping of sacristies; but there are, of course, many variants, the arrangement being dependent on the special parish under consideration.

It may seem that I am assuming a good deal in speaking so assuredly of matters which are as yet by no means common in this country and are only to be found in the few churches where an elaborate ritual is employed, but I am only laying down the most complete scheme that might ever be required. Usage must govern the requirements, and I am concerned only in endeavoring to cover all possible demands. There are few churches, I fancy, where flowers and simple vestments are not used in the service of the altar; and, wherever this is true, a working sacristy is quite as necessary as where a richer ritual is concerned.

The choir sacristy is a comparatively simple matter and needs no description. The priest's sacristy is quite another thing, and demands much thought. Of course, where the simplest ritual is observed, its requirements are comparatively slight; but there are certain things usually demanded, such, for example, as wardrobes for cassocks and surplices, cases for stoles and altar linen, a safe for the storage of the sacred vessels. As the elaborateness of the ritual rises, the demands increase until there must be semicircular cope-cases turning on a central pivot, flat, shallow drawers in great numbers for chasubles, dalmatics, and tunicles, smaller drawers for albs, girdles and maniples. Where all these are necessary, the vestment case may best be arranged with the turning cope-case below, and

LXXV. GREENAWAY'S CHAPEL, TIVERTON CHURCH.

above sliding shelves for chasubles in the middle, with banks of drawers of various sizes on either side. A piscina is most desirable, with its drain, of course, connecting with the soil below the church; and a *prie-Dieu* is imperative. In the centre of the room should be a large table, where vestments may be laid out in preparation for the service.

In Figure LXX. is a good type of sacristy, with its various furnishings arranged as experience has shown desirable.

The priest's sacristy is not a study, neither is it an office. It has its own proper function, and this should be shown in its design and decoration. Domesticity and cosiness are out of

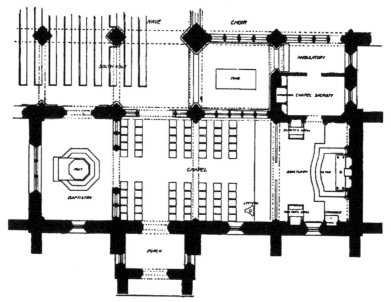

LXXVI. ARRANGEMENT OF CHAPEL AND BAPTISTERY.

the question. The solemnity of the sanctuary pervades it, and in every way this quality should be shown in the treatment.

We have outgrown the curious fancy for looking on a church as simply an auditorium, with a prominent pulpit and a retiring "communion table." While this fancy held, it was appropriate enough, perhaps, to build a preaching hall; but, now that we are arriving at a more just way of looking at things, we are beginning to realize that a church is not a simple problem at all, but instead a thing of the utmost complexity. As I have said before, it should be composed almost like a piece of music. Aisles, ambulatories, chapels, baptisteries, oratories, and even shrines and chantries, all unite to the making of the perfect whole.

I have in mind one church recently completed at great expense. There was a possibility for all the chapels and accessories that any architect could ask, yet the idea of a church as a living thing was utterly forgotten. Not only was the construction of this particular church such as cannot be admitted in religious architecture, but all the chapels that might have been an integral part of a completed whole, adding to it and enhancing its splendor and vitality, were treated in the most casual and accidental fashion. They bear no relation to the church proper, and are without architectural or artistic value of any kind whatever. We cannot afford to make mistakes of this kind.

The problem of church designing is unlike any other that comes before the architect, or rather, perhaps, the difference is in degree. However much it may be necessary for us to consider our architectural problems as studies in united and organized design, it is quite true that in the matter of church building this living quality is supremely dominant. A church is organic; and every line, every mass, every detail, must be carefully considered and perfectly adapted to its ends, forming an essential part of a great and living whole. A church viewed from its architectural standpoint is less a problem of design than a question of what might almost be called creation.

# DECORATION AND STAINED GLASS

Both of these matters are simply problems in design: they fall within the province of the architect, and by him should be determined, precisely as he decides questions of proportion and composition; yet they form so important a category, they fall so naturally into one class, and they are both such fruitful sources of error, that they seem to demand special consideration.

Here in America they have acquired an importance quite out of proportion to their deserts. At least, this is true of decoration, owing to the fact that we are surrounded by churches built, not as those of the Middle Ages, of masonry that is in itself sufficiently decorative, but of materials that have no value in themselves, that are inexpensive, and that simply demand some form of superficial ornamentation. Practically, all of our churches, old or new, are covered with plaster as to their interiors. This is put on in broad masses, and great walls unbroken by mouldings or panel work or carving clamor for some treatment that may give them a degree of beauty. Owing to the disorders and the anarchy of the period of the Reformation and that of the various social and political revolutions that followed from it, nearly every trace of the original color decoration of Christian churches — particularly in those countries where Gothic had reached a high degree of development — has been swept away, and only misleading vestiges remain. With the first awakening of the artistic sense some twenty-five years ago, recourse was had to these fragments for suggestions as to the right course to pursue; and very disastrous were the results.

It is doubtful even if the original thing ever had much value; for, apart from glass-work, the mediæval craftsmen seemed to possess little skill in the use of color, and we have to go back several centuries and seek those countries where Oriental influence asserts itself to find really great color decoration. But, if Gothic color ornamentation was inferior, it was at least better than the modern imitation, which was really just about as bad as could be. At least, it seemed so until something worse took its place. This was the new and presently popular school of Dutch metal and glass beads, Mexican onyx, flashy mosaics, and lacquered brass. For several years this "bar-room" school of decoration ran riot, and the results were utterly lamentable. In Figure LXXXI. is shown an interior of a church that has been ruined by this wave of barbarism, and it is a good example of the disaster that has overtaken scores of once tolerably good churches.

Of course, photographs are almost useless in dealing with this question, for they cannot suggest color, and the color is the most grievous offence; but they can at least show the hopeless triviality of form, the desecration of good lines, the tawdriness, and the vulgarity. In this particular case there was a good foundation,— a simple, finely conceived interior designed by a reserved and conscientious architect. The lines were strong, clean, and graceful, the whole effect grave and self-respecting. Yet the ruthless "decorators," men of fame and position and pretending to authority, went through the thing like a pestilence, and by their absurd fretwork hung on the vaulting, their color, and their frivolous tracery,— above all, by their windows, which violate every law of the art of stained glass,— have metamorphosed a noble church into a cheap auditorium.

This example serves to show the most deadly error that is threatening to-day in the line of decoration, and the one that is

Burne Jones.

LXXVII.  THE ADORATION OF THE MAGI.

most dangerous, since it comes with a certain claim to authority, and, being often an unintelligent imitation of Oriental models, has just that gorgeousness that appeals to the uneducated.

In Figures LXXIX. and LXXX. are examples of really noble decoration, and the contrast between these and the horrible modern imitations, evident enough in photographs, is incalculably more startling in actual fact; for the rank and crude combinations of savage color and cheap gilding of the modern school become in the originals wonderful harmonies that satisfy absolutely.

Perhaps the Capella Palatina (Figure LXXIX.) is the most perfect example of judicious yet magnificent decoration in the world, though in Japan there are temple interiors, particularly that of Chion-in in Kyoto, that press it close. It is jewel work pure and simple; gold and colored mosaic, alabaster, porphyry, opus Alexandrinum and Arabian inlay of nacre and glass mosaic; yet so splendidly is the whole thing composed and tied together, so complete is the reserve in the use of gorgeous materials, that there is no effect of undue richness, not even of ostentation. The result is a great glow of solemn color; and one reverences because one realizes that this is wealth lavished to the glory of God, not to the glorification of men.

The great trouble with modern imitations of this Byzantine and Arabian work is its cheapness. It is an attempt to get effects without paying for them. To copy the decorations of the Capella Palatina to-day would cost hundreds of thousands of dollars, yet plausible tradesmen endeavor to get the optical effect at a tithe of the cost; and the result is — what only it could be — a theatrical and tawdry imitation, irreligious and unworthy.

But this Byzantine splendor of materials is not necessary. In Figure LXXVIII. is a view of one of the best examples of mediæval color decoration that has been preserved to us. This is all pure color, even without gilding; yet the harmony of tone is very wonderful. If we to-day could obtain such results, if we felt color as did Cimabue and Giotto and the subsequent painters down to the time of Tintoretto, it would be safe for us to deal with pigments as they did; but the simple fact is that we do not, and the chances are ten to one that, were we to try to decorate a church after the fashion of this at Assisi, we should fail utterly. We have not the color instinct, and there is the end of it: therefore, the less we try to do in the line of color decoration, the better it will be. Marble we can use, perhaps, as in Figure LXXXII., a wonderful piece of decorative composition; wood-carving also, for we have great carvers in America; stained glass, for we have only to abandon the false prophets of the "picture window," and we shall return to the true school, which is already well established with us. These things we can do; but, in frankness, the less we attempt in the line of decoration of plain surfaces through the use of pigments, the better it will be for us — at present.

In England things are a little better, owing to the fact that there is now established in that happy country a logical and national school of decorative and industrial art. In spite of frequent lapses into frantic sensationalism, there is yet a steady tendency toward better results; and, though the best work is in the line of craftsmanship in metal and wood and needle work, there is yet a certain amount of fine color decoration, as, for example, in Figure LXXXIII This is very original and good: it is not imitated from mediæval or earlier models, but it is thoroughly modern and vital. Yet it is just the sort of thing that, unless it is just right, is likely to be very bad, indeed; and it is not for the hands of the tyro.

LXXVIII. THE UPPER CHURCH AT ASSISI.

LXXIX. THE CAPELLA PALATINA AT PALERMO.

In Figure LXXVII. I have shown a reproduction of what is perhaps the most perfect piece of English ecclesiastical decoration that has thus far been produced, the great tapestry designed by Sir Edward Burne-Jones and executed by William Morris, now hanging in the chapel of Exeter College, Oxford. This most marvellous work has every quality that an ecclesiastical decoration should possess. It is full of the most perfect religious feeling, it is mediæval in its suggestion; yet it is in no way an imitation. It does not pretend to date from the Middle Ages, it is frankly modern; but it is the modernism which must characterize all ecclesiastical art, whether it is architecture, painting, sculpture, or decoration. It is the immutable ideal expressed through modern methods. It is the type of all work of this nature. The spirit which vitalizes it is one which must appear not only in needlework, but in every category of religious art, architecture equally with the others.

But a Burne-Jones and a William Morris appear but seldom under our present civilization. To imitate them is to fail. So the best we can do now is to leave our walls and plain spaces alone, depending on the architecture for our effects. Broad and simple masses of low-toned color are self-respecting and inoffensive, and, above all, safe.

Given a church that architecturally is well composed, strongly massed, simply designed, with lights and shadows well distributed, and the demand for color decoration is not one that is insistent. The sculpture of the reredos, the needlework of altar vestments, the metal of cross and candlesticks and sanctuary lamps, the carving of stalls and pulpit and lectern and organ case, give nearly all the richness, elaboration, and variety that are necessary, while the blazing glass in the windows furnishes the color that the eye demands.

And it is in this last matter — that is, stained glass — that there is the greatest chance for fatal error. For many years we have been told that here in America we make the finest stained glass the world has ever known, and we have accepted this dictum blindly and to our own great injury. The statement contains both truth and falsity. So far as the mere making of colored glass is concerned, there is little cause for complaint: we have produced glass of very wonderful quality and noble color, leaving out of consideration common "cathedral glass," which in its American form is pretty thoroughly bad and in no respect to be compared with that made in England; but further than this one can hardly go in safety. The very wonder of our glass as glass has been our ruin: it has led us hopelessly astray, until nearly all the windows made by fashionable purveyors have been definitely wrong viewed as stained glass, ecclesiastical or otherwise.

The making of stained glass windows is a very noble form of art; but it is decorative art, not pictorial. Any art, to be good, must be based on, even modified by, its own limitations; it must hold itself rigidly to the qualities of its own medium. If it tries to escape from these, it becomes unworthy and without value. All decorative art must be decorative: this is a truism. An easel picture is not primarily decorative, nor yet an isolated statue, but an ecclesiastical fresco, an altar picture, a statue in its niche on a church or any other building, is first of all a piece of decoration; and it must be conceived and executed with a serious regard for its function as a component part of a great whole. This the modern stained glass manufacturer refuses to admit, and at the same time he insists on striving to escape the limitations of his medium. He achieves most wonderful results that make the unthinking public gape; and therefore he exalts his pride, ignorant of the real fact, which is that he has failed of his duty at every point.

LXXX. THE ARCADE OF MONREALE.

LXXXI. MISPLACED DECORATION.

# DECORATION AND STAINED GLASS

Let me quote the published words of a great firm that makes a specialty of what it claims to be ecclesiastical glass : —

" The canons governing the mediævalist are too circumscribed. They would not only hinder the expression of modern artistic aspirations, but also free religious thought. The German and English workers in glass, who have followed exclusively mediæval lines, have found their field of color limited by a symbolism which is largely fanciful, their forms by a conventionalism which is opposed to the intellectual and artistic tendency of the age. ... The result is that windows have been made that far surpass the best ones of the Middle Ages, in color effects so beautiful that they defy description and rival the paintings of the greatest artists, in composition and religious sentiment equal to the best works on canvas."

I think this remarkable statement justifies me in saying that pride has blinded the eyes of glass-stainers to the real nature of what they have done. Nothing, to my mind, could express more exactly all that stained glass is not and should not be.

First of all, then, to enunciate a new doctrine that is yet old,— since it is the governing law of all that was done in this line up to the eighteenth century,— a stained glass window is simply a piece of colored and translucent decoration, absolutely subordinate to its architectural environment, and simply a small component of a great artistic whole. It must continue the structural wall surface perfectly: therefore, it must be flat, without perspective or modelling. It must be decorative and conventional in design and color and in no respect naturalistic. It must never be a hole in a masonry wall, but a portion of that wall made translucent. It must not assert itself; that is, it must hold its place without insolence or insistence. It must be content to be just a means to an end,— no more. In the second place, it is technically a mosaic of pieces of glass; and this it

must always remain. · Great sheets of glass modelled into folds
of drapery are forever forbidden. The glass must be in comparatively small pieces, fastened together by strips of lead of
varying widths; and this leading must be as carefully studied,
as fully respected, as the glass itself. It is not an expedient, an
unfortunate necessity, to be reduced to the smallest size and
quantity: it is of equal honor, of equal importance, with the
glass. To the glowing colors of the quarries it gives the
strength and vigor they would otherwise lack. The treating
of leads as a misfortune to be minimized and concealed is one
of the worst offences of the modern makers of picture windows,
and vitiates their work permanently. If sensationalism in the
use of modelled and opalescent glass is the killing vice of American work, painted glass is very surely an equally deadly sin in
English work. Both violate every law of good glass-making,
both are widely popular, and both are quite unendurable. For
heavily modelled and plated work there is the excuse of startling
and gorgeous effects; for painted work, except so far as slight
touches on hands and faces, there is no excuse whatever.

Another unpardonable corruption is the " picture window."
Certain manufacturers — the great majority, in fact — have taken
to copying in glass the works of the old masters; and the dull
wonder that these triumphs of trickery and bad art have created
has given them a singular vogue. The whole idea is so wrong-
headed, so perverse, so without a possibility of justification, that
it is a waste of time to condemn it in detail. Moreover, adequate space is lacking. It is bad, thoroughly and hopelessly
bad; and that is all one can say.

Almost equally bad are those picture windows that are not
childish copies of pictures new or old, but try to be original
compositions, designs that are full of perspective and modelling,
and that reach over the whole window opening, regardless of

LXXXII. STA. MARIA DEI MIRACOLI, VENICE.

LXXXIII. MODERN ENGLISH DECORATION.

mullions and tracery. As I have said above, perspective and modelling have no place in a window; for it is simply a piece of translucent decoration, flat, rigid, and conventional. Moreover, the mullions are the controlling lines. They circumscribe the decoration absolutely. Beyond their limits a certain subject cannot pass. If they cut a window opening into narrow lights two or three feet wide, as in all Gothic work they must, then the decorative treatment must be calculated for these narrow strips; and beyond these it must not go. The modern and fashionable design that shows clouds and trees and distant rivers and mountains, with people wandering about behind a paling of black mullions, would be grotesque, were it not so indicative of a certain barbarism, and, therefore, tragic.

With that accurate and sensitive grasp of the basic laws of decorative art that marked them above all men except the Japanese, the mediæval glass-workers seized upon the most perfect treatment of the problem, and held to it for centuries. Single figures, each filling the space between two mullions, with the upper portions filled with rich canopy work, is exactly the most frank and decorative treatment that can be discovered; and we can do no better than to adhere to it. Of course, certain subjects adapt themselves to a treatment that ties the window together into a pictorial whole, while yet the various panels remain decoratively distinct. The Annunciation for a double window, and the Resurrection, the Adoration of the Magi, and the Crucifixion for triple windows. But, wherever this pictorial suggestion is used, the utmost care must be taken to see that the work still remains primarily decorative. The figures must be formal, not naturalistic; the backgrounds, decorative, not descriptive; the canopy work should be the same in all the openings, to give unity; and the clothing and vestments should be symbolic.

This latter point is one which is curiously distorted now-adays. We seem to have acquired some of the fear of anything ecclesiastical that hangs over the denominations, and, as well, a passion for misunderstood realism. Therefore, we demand that our Lord and His saints should appear draped in perfectly meaningless folds of clumsy stuff without religious significance, mystic symbolism, or even historical propriety. Now the law of ecclesiastical decoration is that everything should be both decorative and symbolic. Every angel and archangel, every saint, be he martyr or confessor, every prophet, every king, has his proper symbolical vestment and his special attributes. Our Lord Himself, when He is portrayed in glory, is clothed in the splendor of both the royal and the priestly vestments that show forth His twofold glory of Priest and King. The impulse that leads to rebellion against these vestments, these attributes, because of some fancied association, is not one that needs to be considered; for even the Christian style of architecture—nay, even all art itself — falls under the same condemnation.

The mediæval workers in colored glass discovered prac-tically all that there was to know in their art. In the clerestory of Chartres, in the cathedral of Florence, in York minster, to name only a few of the immortal triumphs of glass-making, they reached a point beyond which there was no possibility of further progress. In design, in religious feeling, in decorative quality and workmanship, in the spacing of the quarries and the distribution and proportioning of leads, they said the final word. With all our boasting, we have added nothing to their work. We cannot even make some of the glass they made. We can make very wonderful substitutes that have certain splendid qualities of their own. All we can do is to use this as they would have used it, following implicitly their principles and their ideals.

LXXXIV. AN ENGLISH FIFTEENTH CENTURY WINDOW.

In Figure LXXXIV. I have shown a reproduction of a very beautiful fifteenth-century window, which I have taken from a most admirable article on stained glass in the *Architectural Re-*

Reginald Hallward.
LXXXV. DECORATION OF ROOF.

*view*, written by Mr. Otto Heinigke, of the firm of Heinigke & Bowen, and in Figure LXXXVI. have shown a modern English design, which I do not hesitate to call a piece of the most masterly leading, and as well of stained glass designing that cannot be criticised in any way.

It may seem to some that I have devoted an undue amount of space to the consideration of stained glass, also that I have been too severe in my condemnation of a school which is widely

Gerald Moira.

LXXXVI. EXAMPLE OF GOOD LEADED GLASS.

popular with us to-day; but stained glass is inseparable from Gothic architecture, the two are absolutely united. No matter how good the church, it may be quite ruined by false glass; and, on the other hand, glass rightly conceived may do much toward saving many a structure. For the technical triumphs of the popular glass-makers I have every admiration, but I have tried in vain to obtain from some of them designs worked out after established precedents. I have found myself compelled to take what they saw fit to give,— that is, "picture windows,"— or go elsewhere. Now in any Gothic church a picture window is finally impossible. If the famous glass-makers will recog-

LXXXVII. NEWCASTLE CATHEDRAL.

nize this fact, and will show their willingness to do work which will be consistent with the style, religious in spirit, and purely decorative in treatment, then the architects can ask nothing better.

To show the false position the art of glass-staining occupies nowadays, let me speak of an incredible occurrence I know of. Certain people who were proposing to give a memorial window, and who had a liking for the painter Millet, asked a certain firm of glass-stainers to make a window representing "The Sower"; and, instead of refusing the commission, it was accepted with alacrity. Now no subject could possibly be chosen which was less adaptable to stained glass than this particular picture; and yet the work was cheerfully undertaken, without the least regard to the absurdity of the idea. Not only this, but, at the instigation of the donors, the glass-makers copied the well-known picture; and, because the man in whose memory the window was to be erected wore a beard, they showed this beard on Millet's figure. Could anything be more preposterous and more disheartening? Yet this is an example of what is asked for, and what is gotten at this time; and it shows how totally false is the attitude of the public and the makers of glass toward this most noble and exalted form of religious art.

# THE ALTAR

As the altar is the church, as it is the reason for the existence of the wonderful fabric that has gradually developed into
the most exalted and highly organized of the buildings of men,
so is it from an architectural standpoint the centre, the climax
of the structural church. To it all things are tributary; and
whether you say that the church itself flows from it as from the
centre of life, or that the visible organism develops cell by cell,
until it completes itself in that for which it exists, in that which
is the object of its being, the result is the same. The altar
stands forth as the great dominating energy that controls
and vitalizes all: it is the soul of the marvellous organism
that is as nearly a living thing as anything man is permitted
to create.

In designing a church, this one thing must always be held
in mind. Every line, every mass, every detail, is so conceived
and disposed that it exalts the altar, that leads to it, as any
work of art leads to its just climax. By the lines of arcades,
the curves of arch and vault, the ranged windows, and the
gathering chapels and aisles with their varied lights and
shadows, the eye, and through the eye the mind, and through
the mind the soul, is led onward step by step until it rests on
the altar itself. (See Figure LXXXVII.)

A good church, like any work of good art, is one that is so
delicately organized, so finely differentiated, that it almost lives.
To the simpler forms of building it bears the same relation
that man bears to the lower forms of life; and, like man, it possesses that which raises it immeasurably above every other
organism, a soul, and that soul is the altar.

Yet in itself this is but a simple stone of small size, too

insignificant in point of mere dimensions to serve as the dominating motive in a great church.   Therefore, we surround it
with accessories of great richness, that serve as steps from the
highest elaboration we are able to obtain in the structure of
the church to the centre of all things.   From moulded and
carven arches, niches with their statues, and traceried windows
glowing with color, we pass to the intricate fretwork of canopied stalls, finely wrought wainscot and walls of tapestry and
gilded leather, until we reach the reredos, the splendid frame-
work of the altar, the ultimate richness of the entire church,
where is concentrated all the ornamentation that our means
afford.   Then there is one more step to the altar itself; and
where a church is treated as a living whole, as a splendid and
perfect organism, everything concentrates in a point of the
most faultless splendor, in altar vestments of intricate needlework wrought in colors and gold, in candlesticks of goldsmith's
work, in a jewelled cross, and, finally, and supremely, in that
which is the glowing point where everything centres at last,
the chalice.

The man who, when he thinks of designing a church, does
not halt abashed and ashamed before the tremendous responsibility that confronts him, has not yet learned how to build a
church; and, when he does understand, it may perhaps happen
that he will meet with a refusal when he asks permission to so
design his work that it may have that organic quality that lives.
Only too often he will find certain rules arbitrarily made for
him which will bring all his labors to naught.   Our failure
to achieve good results in church building nowadays is very
largely due to our inability to see that a church is an entity in
itself, that it is even more a thing of immutable law than a
musical composition, that it must be conceived as a whole, and
that it has one central fact that inexorably conditions every-

LXXXVIII. REREDOS, ALL SAINTS', DORCHESTER.

LXXXIX. CHANCEL, TRINITY CHURCH, BOSTON.

XC. TRINITY CHURCH, NEW YORK.

thing else, to which all is subject, by which all is tested; and that central fact is the altar.

I have in mind one church that is a good example of the death that overtakes a work of ecclesiastical art when the principle of unity, when the idea of climax, of culmination, is abandoned. The cost was enormous, the richness of decoration seldom equalled in modern times. The choir and sanctuary are those of a cathedral, vast and imposing; and in the midst, raised on a single step, stands a black walnut table of small size, innocent of vestments, of candles, of flowers, without a suggestion of reredos, barren even of the Cross of our Redemption. The whole design of the church demands a lofty altar under a towering baldacchino, with marble columns supporting a marble dome. With this the fabric would live: without it, it is dead. (See Figure LXXXIX.)

For, when the altar and its reredos are raised in a church, then the fabric receives the breath of life. I am speaking architecturally. As an architect, I have no concern with schools of Churchmanship; but, as an architect, I am privileged to say that, unless the altar is treated with due regard, unless it has its proper relation to the rest of the fabric, then every effort to obtain a church that is a living thing is vain, and worse than vain.

For, if we consider a church as an organism, we shall realize that both in dimensions and in degree of richness there is a certain proportion that must be observed. The height of the foot-pace must bear a certain relation to the height of the church, the length of the altar to the width of the sanctuary, the dimensions of the reredos to the length of the church and the size of the east wall, the richness of decoration to that which obtains elsewhere in the church. It is not a question of ritual: it is a question of art; and, as a question of art, it is also a

XCI. REREDOS, MERTON CHAPEL, OXFORD.

question of religion, since art, in the service of the Church, is simply art as an incentive to religious emotion.

XCII. TRIPTYCH, CHURCH AT PENDLEBURY.

Let us consider, a little more in detail, the matter of the design of the altar and its reredos.

Of the altar there is very little to be said, further than that it must be of stone and that its length must bear its proper relation to the size of the church. For the principal or " high

159

altar" a length of less than eight feet is practically out of the
question, since this length can hardly be less than a third of the
width of the sanctuary in a Gothic church. Neither can this
length well exceed twelve feet, since the height is fixed at three
feet four inches; and greater length gives an effect of unpleasant
thinness. The depth need be scarcely more than two feet. The
foot-pace must be as broad as possible, particularly if the altar is
ever to be served by priest, deacon, and sub-deacon. In this case,
also, the steps must be sufficiently wide for a minister to stand on
each of them easily. More than five steps from the floor of the
sanctuary to the foot-pace are awkward; and, if greater elevation
is necessary, this can be obtained by steps in the choir or, better
still, when the sanctuary is deep enough, by additional steps inside the communion rail. If possible, the altar should stand out
from the reredos, giving a space behind for convenience in ar-
ranging candlesticks and flowers on the retables, which are, of
course, a part of the reredos, not of the altar.

Whether the altar front shall be rich with sculpture and
mosaic and precious marbles, or whether it shall be quite plain
and covered with embroidered frontals, is a matter of ritual, not
of architecture.

It is in the reredos that the great opportunity for splendor
of design offers itself, and the possible variations are almost
endless. The earliest form is that of the baldacchino, a canopy
of some kind supported on columns; but when, with the development of a purely Christian style of architecture, the altar
found its place against the east wall, this form was abandoned
for that of the great screen of canopied niches, richly sculptured
panels, and fretted pinnacles. It was in the fifteenth century,
and in England, that this wonderful creation of the mediæval
builders reached its highest development; and, though nearly all
were shattered and wrecked by those acting under the authority

H. Wilson, Architect.

XCIII.  TRIPTYCH, DOUGLASS CASTLE.

XCIV. REREDOS, GLASGOW CATHEDRAL.

of Henry VIII. and Oliver Cromwell, many have been well restored, and stand as monuments of an age that was great in
Christian art.

Probably that of Winchester cathedral (Frontispiece) is
the noblest of them all, both in its general conception and in
its detail; and it has served as a model for many that have followed both in its own country and under the restoration that is
taking place in ours. Roughly speaking, there are three types
of reredos, — the sculptured screen either joined to the east wall
or detached from it (Frontispiece and Figure LXXXVIII.), the
niched wall where the entire space is covered with decoration
(Figure XCI.), and the triptych (Figures XCII., XCIII.). In
the cases of the screen and the triptych there may be a window
above or behind the reredos. Sometimes the latter rises well
over the windows, showing the flicker of colored light through
its pierced tracery and carving; and, when this is done, the
effect may be most beautiful. The niched wall is seldom found
except in chapels, and is too lacking in composition and concentration to commend itself. The triptych is also more appropriate for side chapels than for any high altar, since its size
must always be limited. It is a very mobile form, however, and
offers great opportunities for the most splendid effects of inlay,
color, and gold. It may easily be made exceedingly bad, as can
be seen in Figure XCII., which is as ill-designed as Figure
XCIII. is nobly conceived. Of course, the triptych demands
good pictures; and religious painting is so nearly a lost art nowadays that it is almost out of the question.

The sculptured screen, some modification of the typical
Winchester screen, remains the best and safest form; but it
must be carefully designed, and with great gravity and restraint,
for it will tend to the condition of the frivolous, "gingerbready"
follies that at present seem to affect the altar designs of the

Roman Church. Just how to strike a balance between the necessary architectural quality and the quality of sculpture is a difficult task. The tendency is apt to be too strong in either direction. In Figure XCIV. the effect is thoroughly bad, just because the whole thing is too coldly architectural: it is a structural episode with no relation to the altar or anything else, Figure XCV. errs in just the other direction: it is trivial, and stamped with the mark of the wedding confection. The reredos shown in the frontispiece remains the perfect type, for it is at the same time architectural and "sculpturesque." Its proportions are faultless, its composition masterly, its arrangement of light and shade as perfect as anything left us from mediæval times. Now that the long empty cross has received its Figure of our Lord, and the interpolated picture has given place to the original range of small statues, the reredos, completely restored, takes its place as one of the most perfect achievements of Christian architecture.

Another form of reredos, and one seen but infrequently, is that which has the screen form, but is made of wood and decorated with the color and gold of the triptych. That in the chapel of St. Paul's School, Concord, N.H., by Mr. Vaughan (Figure XCVI.), is undoubtedly the finest of these; and its effect of sonorous color and splendid light is most satisfying.

Where by reason of the necessarily great cost a reredos is temporarily out of the question the dossal gives the requisite emphasis and the effect of honor that are indispensable. The dossal that consists of a flat curtain of vertical strips of alternating brocade and some plain and rich material, a projecting canopy or "lambrequin," and wings of a stuff somewhat lighter in weight, is by far the the best form. A dossal that hangs in folds has too much the effect of upholstery, and it lacks the dignity so requisite. Without the projecting canopy the effect

XCV. ALTAR AND REREDOS, ST. PATRICK'S CATHEDRAL, NEW YORK.

Henry Vaughn, Architect.

XCVI. REREDOS, CHAPEL OF ST. PAUL'S SCHOOL, CONCORD, N. H.

XCVII ALTAR BRASSES, ALL SAINTS, DORCHESTER, MASS.

is apt to be too flat and bald. Of course the dossal is suscep-
tible of the utmost enrichment in the way of embroidery, if this
is desired. Where a reredos that is absolutely right in richness
and elaboration is impossible, it is far better to rely on some
form of dossal than to compromise on a small, insignificant, or
barren makeshift. By the very nature of its place and its function a reredos *must* be rich and splendid, the best of its kind;
and the best costs very much, which is not true of fabrics
where a few hundred dollars will obtain something that is
really precious in itself.

Of the frontals and superfrontals it may be said that the
majority of modern examples err in that they are too often conceived simply as pieces of embroidery, not as integral parts of
an architectural *ensemble*. One constantly sees elaborate pieces
of embroidery where the work is faultless, where even the detail of the design is good, but where just this lack of architectural quality is fatal. Strong lines, broad masses, powerful
color composition, are all most necessary; and without these
qualities faithful and elaborate workmanship and precious
materials go for nothing. Some of the very best examples are
simply intelligent combinations of panels of heavy brocade with
orphreys of plain velvet; and this is just because the brocade or
damask has the formality of pattern and the decorative design
that are imperative.

But this matter of ecclesiastical embroidery is one that should
be treated in a separate book, the subject is so involved and
elaborate. I speak of it here simply from a desire to emphasize
the fact that it must of necessity be conceived in relation to its
position, that it must be treated as a part of an architectural
or, rather, artistic composition.

The same is true of the altar brasses, crosses, candlesticks,
and vases, and of the sacred vessels. It is almost impossible

to get the former in any really good design unless they are especially made. They are too often crude in design, tawdry in effect, and rough in workmanship. The common trade-stuff of "spun" brass, thin and cheap but brilliantly lacquered, is just as bad as it can possibly be. It is strange that people do not understand that anything that touches the altar or is used in honoring it *must* be absolutely as good, both in workmanship and design, as man can create. Cheapness and show are banished forever from the sanctuary.

XCVIII. TRIPTYCH IN PAINTED PLASTER. R. Anning Bell.

# THE CATHEDRAL

As the altar is the centre, the culmination, of each individual church, the focus of honor, where all the powers of art concentrate to exalt into visible dignity that which is in itself the supreme wonder of the universe, so is the cathedral the centre and culmination of the whole Church. It is the embodiment of no greater glory than that which makes the least of chapels a Tabernacle of God; but it is a certain sign of the unity and dominion of the visible Church, and as the place of the cathedra of a bishop it acquires a certain dignity supplementary to that which marks the parish church. But it is more than this: a cathedral is not only the chief church of a diocese, the bishop's church, it is also the embodiment of the Church militant, the manifestation of the visible Church, the type and symbol of the Church triumphant. Its significance is more than official, its importance other than administrative. It is the church not only of the bishop, but of every soul within his jurisdiction; it is the common meeting-ground of all, the centre of light and education and evangelical energy; it is the heart and brain of the ecclesiastical organism. Structurally it is the work of generations of men striving to show forth in some sort the glory of the heavenly city, the power of the Church triumphant, the majesty and dominion of the kingdom of God.

It is true that any church where the bishop establishes his throne becomes *ipso facto* a cathedral; but the cathedral idea is more than this. A parish church, even if of great size and splendor, does not fulfil the requirement. It may serve as a pro-cathedral; but unless it is conceived architecturally on cathedral lines, unless it begins to grow glorious through an endless series of benefactions, unless it becomes indeed a centre of vitality for the whole diocese, it remains but a pro-cathedral still. For the cathedral is more the expression of an idea than a function; and, while it must be adapted to the latter, it must be conceived and worked out with a very careful regard to the former quality, which is very evidently of equal importance. If we consider the cathedrals of the past, in whatever country they may be found, we shall see how almost invariably the old builders worked with this thought in mind, and, if they labored unconsciously, were inevitably driven by impulse to attain the same ends. During the whole period of the Middle Ages, when the Church reached her highest degree of development and power, the cathedrals were designed in a fashion that differentiated them completely from parish churches, however large and gorgeous those may have been, while they bore no close resemblance to the abbey churches and monastery chapels. The cathedral was a special structure, with its own laws, its own qualities; and as such it was conceived.

Here and there, of course, there were exceptions to this rule; and we sometimes find the cathedral to be but an insignificant structure, the chief church in the city but the chapel of some civil or ecclesiastical authority, as in Venice or Rome; but, wherever this occurs, there was some special and local reason, the normal condition was one where the cathedral was not only the crowning glory of the diocese, but of the civil State as well.

It was during the Middle Ages, while the Gothic, or Christian, style of architecture was supreme, that the cathedral idea received its fullest development; and, therefore, the greatest cathedrals are fortunately in this style. The Roman basilicas that preceded them were prevented by the hampering conditions of their style from expressing the great and growing idea to the full, and the Romanesque temples that followed were equally

XCIX. DURHAM.

handicapped. St. Peter's in Rome, though not a diocesan cathedral, and St. Paul's in London, are not the structures we turn to for the most perfect embodiment of the idea of the Church in its glory, but rather Chartres and Amiens, Seville and Bourges, Durham and York and Gloucester and Lincoln (See Figures XCIX., C., CI., and CII.). San Marco seems but what it was designed to be, a gorgeous and wonderful chapel, the Renaissance edifices are but theatrical and pretentious affectations, while many of the small cathedrals of England are such only by virtue of the fiat of the bishop,— by intention and in effect they are but parish churches or monastery chapels; but the real cathedrals, the awful fabrics of chiselled stone, with their solemn and cavernous interiors, the monuments of Christian civilization from the eleventh to the sixteenth centuries, are, and must forever remain, unmatched evidences of the dignity and the dominion of the visible Church, of the imperishable glories of the Church triumphant.

 When the Church in England began to enter into her new life after the dark ages that came upon her with the Civil Wars and the resulting Commonwealth, it was the administrative aspect of the edifice that asserted itself rather than that higher symbolical quality; and, therefore, it is natural, of course, that this same idea should have obtained here in America. " The bishop's church," — this was at first all it was held to be,— a parish church selected from among those of the diocesan city and made into a cathedral by the addition of a throne; or else a new structure a little richer and more elaborate, with certain reminiscent suggestions of the English prototype, only made small and ineffectual. This idea was wholly wrong, but it was only temporary; and, since the cathedral at Albany was projected and begun, there has been no excuse for any failure to work on the ancient lines. One may criticise the style of Albany, perhaps,

C. LINCOLN.

Cl. GLOUCESTER.

as one must criticise the style of the New York cathedral; but the impelling motive was right, and the name of the bishop of Albany will always be remembered as that of the prelate who was primarily responsible for the introduction into the Church in America of the true cathedral idea. There is no longer any excuse for such blunders as the cathedral at Garden City. In future, whatever is done must be done right.

And what is this "right"? We have but to look back through England and France, and we shall see. I have already tried to indicate the spiritual significance of the cathedral. How shall we best work this out in visible form?

First of all, by realizing that a cathedral is a structure to be erected for all time and for an entire diocese; that it must be dependent in no respect on temporary conditions, but that it must be so planned that, as years go by, something may be added, until a century hence, perhaps, the fabric will stand completed,—so far, that is, as its mere structure is concerned. It must always remain a nucleus for constant additions of chapel and tomb and oratory, windows, statues, and pictures. The cathedral is never finished; it is a record of advancing years forever without term. To build temporarily, to abandon and rebuild elsewhere, is to forsake the whole idea of the cathedral as a type of the everlasting Church. Let us suppose that some one of the smaller dioceses reaches a point where a cathedral is desired. There is available the sum of, perhaps, $100,000. What would be the ordinary course? To build as large an edifice, complete except for towers and decoration, as could be obtained for the money. And this would be a negation of the whole cathedral idea. Rather should this be done. Lay out roughly the scheme of a vast and imposing structure, then begin one small section and finish this up to a point where it could be used, if, as with us is almost inevitable, the cathedral

CII. YORK MINSTER, FROM THE SOUTH-WEST.

is also a parish church. If there is money enough, build the great choir, or carry the walls up part way, putting on a temporary roof. If this is too much, then build simply the crypt and use that for the time being. "But such a structure would be ugly, an eyesore, perhaps for years." What of that? You are not erecting a church for your own admiration, for the self-satisfaction of the worshippers therein. You are laying the first stones of a witness to the glory of God, and the foundations of a mighty temple, always more honorable than the complete walls of a third-rate fabric. In the unhewn stones and blunted walls of Albany, in the crags of monstrous masonry of New York, there is glory and honor; but in the small trivialities, the cast-iron expedients, of Garden City there is nothing of either of these.

If it is true that a parish church is only secondarily an auditorium, and that its greatness as a house of worship must not be sacrificed to its requirements as a house of instruction, it is also true that a cathedral is not even secondarily an auditorium. We may compromise in a parish church, but in a cathedral not at all. If we build aright,— that is, if we build in the Christian style and as the men of the Middle Ages built,— we shall have good acoustics, and this is all we can ask; to ruin a fabric as a temple of God wrought with all the strength of exalted art by trying to give every seat a clear view of the pulpit, or by abandoning aisles and chapels and great piers of masonry, is to be guilty of great foolishness. All that a parish church must be holds in the case of a cathedral, and more, immeasurably more. The qualities of grandeur and sublimity, of mystery and awe, of shadow and silence, of eternal durability and wealth of ornamentation paid for by willing sacrifice,— all these things must be almost as the corner-stone: they must exist, or the labor is in vain. To obtain them, we must abandon some questions of

CIII. AMIENS.

practicability, of economy of space; but such action needs no defence: he who would question it has failed to lay hold of the meaning of the Church.

A cathedral is not a structural necessity, it is not a measure of convenience. Its justification is higher: it is the most highly evolved and the most perfect of the fabrics conceived by man, reared as a standing testimony of the impulses of reverence, faith, and devotion that animate the Church. It is untouched by materialism and commercialism: it is purely ideal; and, as in the past, so now it is the crowning work of man dedicated to the enduring glory of God.

There is no reason why the smallest diocese should not lay the first stones of the greatest cathedral: numbers do not count, but faith and devotion. The good cathedrals of the Middle Ages stand, many of them, in little villages, or at least in small cities that have never been larger and expect no greater future. Such, for example, are Ely and Peterborough, Wells and Salisbury and Gloucester; and they are the more wonderful for the very fact that they *do* stand in such places. They are beacons of salvation, enduring monuments of centuries of living piety; and they rise from the midst of clustering cottages or village shops, cities of God, set indeed on a hill, shining with a light that shall not be hid.

Before we consider the matter of the contemporary cathedral, let us look at one or two of the most triumphant monuments of the past. They are the type that we must follow in every way. The Church has not changed, nor the requirements of a cathedral; nor, so far as we in this country are concerned, has the race been so modified as to demand new modes of expression. The Church in England and her architectural style are our own, and none can deprive us of our birthright.

There are, then, two great types of the Gothic cathedral, the French and the English. All the others — Spanish, German, and Flemish — are only modifications of the original French type. Each method has its own virtues, its own defects. The French cathedral stands first in point of sublimity of conception and unity of effect, also in overwhelming grandeur, in emotional power, and in the perfect working out from a structural standpoint of the great Christian style of architecture. The English cathedral stands first in point of spontaneity, of quiet sincerity, of personal devotion. Rheims, Amiens,

CIV. EXETER.

Chartres, while unmatched in their awful glory, have yet something of pride, even self-consciousness. They proclaim rather the infinite majesty and the royal dominion of God than the loving-kindness that is declared by Winchester, Exeter, Lincoln, and Wells. (See Figures C., CV., and CIV.) I do not mean this as a criticism of the French type, but only as a differentiation. From an abstract architectural standpoint the French cathedrals are far more perfect than the English;

CV. WINCHESTER.

but in their very pride of acknowledged power, in their dazzling perfection, there is something that incites almost foreboding. Consummate achievement treads the perilous edge of catas-trophe, and in the very faultlessness of Amiens lies the threat of the ignominy of Beauvais.

In England, on the other hand, there is no trace of the pride that goeth before a fall. The builders of the cathedrals were not masterly men. They dared not pile their stones to the dizzy

CVI. BEAUVAIS—EXTERIOR OF CHOIR.

heights that lured the French. They shrank from cutting away the supports until the stone vaults hung breathlessly in the air. They did not understand how to dispose of columns, how to trace the lines of aisles and chapels, how to curve their arches and vaults as best to obtain the most awe-inspiring effects of shadow and fluctuant light and misty, bewildering perspective. And, just because they did not, they often achieved a success equal to, if not beyond, that of their more self-conscious rivals on the Continent. Moreover, while the French cathedrals, even if built during several centuries, show yet a certain unity of design, those of England are usually without the least architectural consistency; for they show the mutations of style, the vicissitudes of society, the march of history, the personality of their builders, in a most eminent degree. France is full of matchless architectural monuments, but England's whole history is writ large in her churches.

It is fortunate for her that this is so. Wherever we find a church complete in any one given style, as Salisbury, for example (Figure CVIII.), we find comparative failure. Here the plan is almost beyond criticism, the general grouping and composition finely conceived; and yet the result is thin and dry and poor, and Salisbury stands as one of the least good of English cathedrals. This is partly due to the fact that the style, "Early English," was not one of any great degree of beauty, being crude, hard, and undeveloped, and partly to the offices of the unspeakable Wyatt, who in the eighteenth century swept away every trace of subsequent additions in the shape of chapels, chantries, screens, and tombs, leaving the fabric forlorn in all its nakedness. But the fact remains that never have the English achieved the greatness of idea that impelled the French, where, on the other hand, they have wrought into enduring stone a personality that is very precious. Before Chartres one is dumb with awe, and a little afraid; but Durham and Peterborough, though the most solemn and imposing of the cathedrals of England, create only feelings of love, kinship, and personal affection.

In the French type the general scheme is of the simplest, the

component parts equally simple. The root is composed of the
nave and transepts crossing and forming a Latin cross. Outside this comes an aisle completely surrounding the main fabric,
and at the east end a further sequence of polygonal chapels

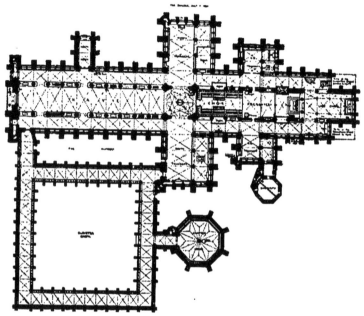

CVII. SALISBURY—PLAN.

forming the chevet. Occasionally these chapels are continued
down each side of the nave; and now and then, as in Cologne,
this line of subsidiary chapels becomes a perfect aisle. The
extreme contour of the plan is perfectly simple, symmetrical,
and unbroken. (Figure CIX.) The entire fabric is vaulted in
stone; and the thrust of these vaults is received by flying buttresses, made necessary by the fact that the system of construc-

CVIII. SALISBURY.

tion, which is that of concentrated loads, renders solid buttresses impossible. The height of the central nave is from
three to four times the width. Viewed simply as an architectural product, the French cathedral is seen to be the most mar-

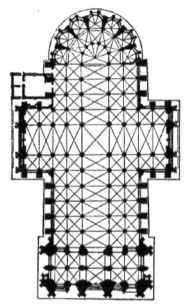

Cologne Cathedral, Germany. 13th Century.

CIX. COLOGNE—PLAN.

vellous work of man. It is almost a living organism : every stone,
every arch, every foot of wall, is designed with an almost un-
imaginable degree of scientific knowledge. Each part has its
function. Nothing is wasted, nothing is unnecessary. It grows
like a living thing, and stands unmatched among the material
products of man's intelligence.

And the resulting effect from an emotional and artistic

CX. NOTRE DAME—WEST FRONT.

standpoint is only what must follow from anything conceived in this masterly fashion. One kneels in Chartres, Amiens, Rheims, dumb and breathless, awed by the indescribable majesty, dazed by the triumph of the human mind; and yet — is it the quickening of a national soul, the answering of blood to blood, the

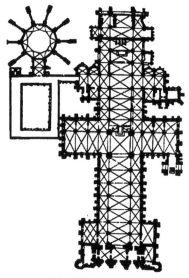

CXI. LINCOLN—PLAN.

thrill of indestructible kinship? Something of all of these, perhaps; for it is not to be denied that from the awful majesty of France one turns to the brave, humble, struggling sincerity of England as a son to his forgotten patrimony.

And this is well. We may admit the supremacy of the French Gothic cathedrals, but they are not for us. The English is ours; for we two are one people, with one history and one blood.

I do not mean that we must be imitative or archæological. We may take what we will from France or Spain or Flanders;

CXII. CANTERBURY.

but let us apply it all to the English root, so creating a thing that is racial and — our own.

For I believe that in the varied plans of the English cathedrals is the germ of even greater things than have been wrought in France. The French cathedral is Greek in its perfect simplicity of idea, mediæval in the infinite variety and richness of its detail. In England was conceived an idea more original, more supple, capable of far greater mobility of treatment. Durham, Lincoln, and Salisbury are good examples. (See Figures CVII. and CXI.)

Inadequate, chaotic, undeveloped, there is yet visible a possibility that is almost unlimited. It was never fully worked out. It is still rudimentary, but — it exists. The central and dominating tower is a logical development, full of vast possibilities. The square-ended choir makes possible effects unattainable on an apsidal plan. The secondary, eastern transept is a stroke of genius; the multiplication of chapels and chantries, the grouping of cloister, chapter house, and subsidiary buildings, full of wonderful opportunities. Then, again, in England was conceived that marvellous thing, fan-vaulting; while only there did Gothic succeed in taking to itself certain qualities of the good, early Renaissance, and in assimilating them.

Let us admit at once that England never succeeded in thoroughly working out the cathedral idea on the lines she had indicated for herself. Externally good, the central tower was never wholly right inside; and the only attempt at a new solution of the problem, Ely, was not a success.

Unity yielded, and historic continuity, and the Reformation destroyed all artistic and religious development just at the time when there seemed a chance that a great, consistent English cathedral might come into being. The Chapel of Henry VII. is a suggestion of what might have been, but, like nearly all English work, only a suggestion.

Gothic in England was a living and constantly developing style. It was full of immense vitality, personality. Its growth was suddenly arrested, and then all artistic labor ceased. The sequence is once more constituted, and it is for us to take up the work once abandoned until better days.

CXIII. ALBANY CATHEDRAL.

CXIV. COMPETITIVE DESIGN, NEW YORK CATHEDRAL.

In the modern cathedral, the fabric of to-day, built in a new land as the chief church and seat of the bishop's throne, in some diocese that counts at best but little more than a century since its foundation, we find, as I have already said, the most perfect opportunity that ever presents itself to an architect. I have tried to show why church building is the most noble, the most exalted, and the most perfect of the functions of architecture ; and it follows of course from this that the cathedral, the culminating point of the structural church, is the problem that possesses the greatest possibilities. It is a task before which every man must halt abashed. Not only must the result of his labors do honor to the Church herself, but as well it must find itself contrasted with the triumphant monuments of the great past ; and thus far the contrast has always resulted to the discredit of the modern work. In this lies failure and reproach, not only to architecture, but to the Church herself. Yet, confronted by reiterated failure, the architect must still go on, striving always for something better, looking always toward the possible time when at last the restoration of civilization may make possible the production through him of that temple that shall mark a corresponding restoration of the continuity that has so long been broken.

It is not an easy task. Three centuries of architectural dark ages have left us rather blind and helpless, knowing not where to turn ; and, without disrespect, we may say with equal truth that the same three centuries have resulted in removing from the Church herself the impulse and the wisdom that might otherwise have directed us. The cathedral of Albany was at least conceived on the right lines, but this was due rather to the incentive of one prelate than to a general recrudescence of the right idea throughout the Church. When the competition for the New York cathedral was held, we saw at once how blind were the gropings, both of the Church and of the architects. Practically, none of the designs submitted showed the least appreciation of the cathedral idea; and the variation was from the dry and coldly mechanical (Figure CXIV.) through the crudely unintelligent (Figure CXV.) to the mad and fantastically

CXV. COMPETITIVE DESIGN, NEW YORK CATHEDRAL.

impossible (Figure CXVI.). It was the chance of a century, and none came forward to seize upon it to the glory of the Church and to his own immortality.

This experience in America was only a repetition of that in England, and it had far greater excuse; for, when there was a project of building a cathedral in Liverpool, and a competition was held, there were great church builders in England, and yet no designs remotely approached meeting the demands of the situation, though of course the general average was much higher than with us. Very wisely, the Liverpool project was dropped.

Halsey Wood.
CXVI. COMPETITIVE DESIGN, NEW YORK CATHEDRAL.

Were it to be taken up again now, the results would be very different.

The only two important modern cathedrals in Great Britain are those of Truro (Figure CXVII.) and Belfast (Figure

197

CXVIII.); and both, while conceived in dignity and with something of the cathedral idea, are yet dry and archæological, both attempted restorations of dead styles,— Truro of the Early English, Belfast of the Decorated. Neither shows a touch of vitality in point of architectural style; and, therefore, both of them either

CXVII. TRURO CATHEDRAL.

prove the same lack in the Church or else they are slanderous misrepresentations.

Of course, they date from some years back, and are no proof of what might be possible now, and the same is true of Albany and New York; but, while we have a new confidence in England based on the work of such powerful and well-advised men as Bodley & Garner, Paley & Austin, and Leonard Stokes, have we that assurance here? Certainly not, if we are to judge from the two designs once tentatively put out for the ultimately possible Washington cathedral, one of which was actually Roman Renaissance in style, the other an archæological French

CXVIII. BELFAST CATHEDRAL.

Gothic, both vacant of any hint of the history and the nature of the Anglican Communion of the Catholic Church in America. Yet we have men here who are able to design a great cathedral: the trouble is, that it is the others who, for some reason or other, obtain the opportunity.

Such "cathedrals" as we now possess, with the single ex-

CXIX. GARDEN CITY CATHEDRAL.

ception of Albany, need hardly be referred to; for, if we leave out Long Island, they are all merely parish churches, or pro-cathedrals. Garden City may be used simply as an example of every single thing in design and construction that should be piously shunned. It is a cheap and frivolous toy, and as a toy to be avoided. (See Figure CXIX.)

Recently a beginning has been made on a cathedral in Cleveland (Figure CXX.). Apart from the almost fatal defect of small scale, the dimensions being those of a parish church, the scheme is by no means unworthy of the cathedral idea. The architect, Mr. C. F. Schweinfurth, has succeeded in obtaining a certain dignity and cathedral effect in spite of hampering conditions. With one more bay added to the length, with the nave extended to the street line over the narthex, with ten feet added to the interior height and twenty to the tower, the design, except in point of style, perhaps, would be admirable. Still, the fact remains that we have not as yet seized upon the true cathedral idea in this country. Where one like the bishop of Albany, and he the first in America, lays hold of the true idea, he is able only to a limited degree to convey to his architect the principle he himself has so clearly in mind. When an almost unrivalled opportunity offers, as in New York, no architect comes forward to seize upon it and make it his own. When even this great chance is excelled by another, the projected Washington cathedral, the first published suggestions are confused and made of no account by fictitious ideas of a supposed necessity for a certain architectural harmony with the existing buildings of the civil government, or else by an equally fictitious theory as to the advisability of employing the most highly developed form of the Christian style without regard to ecclesiastical history or ethnic development.

When a vast sum becomes available by bequest, as in the

case of Garden City, careless and uncultured executors turn a sacred trust into a commercial operation, and carry out the terms of the bequest with absolutely no regard for architectural or ecclesiastical principles.

When, as in Cleveland, the motive is just, the idea noble, the conception absolutely right, the whole goes for naught

C. F. Schweinfurth, Architect.

CXX. CLEVELAND CATHEDRAL.

through the failure to recognize one of the most essential qualities of a cathedral,— namely, its eternity; and, therefore, short-sighted schemes of temporary economy and rapid completion hamper the architect, and result in the building of but one more pro-cathedral. Yet, through all our failures, we can see something of progress. If one cathedral can be begun with the right ideals of Albany and New York as the foundation, and with the addition of an equally right architectural style, there will be little chance of a relapse into our former unenlightened state. For this reason the projected Washington cathedral is a thing of unmatched importance. Albany and New York are fixed in style, the former irrevocably, the latter subject to modification in detail that, apparently, is taking place very rapidly and in the right direction; but Washington is still an open question. Solved rightly, it may be the beginning of a radical architectural revolution, the results of which are incalculable. Solved amiss,— that is, as a problem in archæological erudition, Roman or French,— it will mean harm immeasurable and the postponing of the needed architectural reform for many years.

What is this correct solution? What relation does the modern cathedral bear to that of mediævalism? What of the ancient qualities persist, what have ceased, what new things have been added?

First of all, those supreme qualities of ultimate grandeur and sublimity already postulated for the parish church by reason of its nature as a Tabernacle of the Living God, those qualities which are to be obtained through self-sacrifice and through the giving of the absolute best we have in art and labor, are as persistent now as in the past. Then, also, we must build in such wise as to crush with awe all those who enter the portals, and raise them again into spiritual exaltation. We must build for all time and little by little, making what is to-day but one minor cell, perhaps, in the final vast and triumphant organism. We must so design the work that it will best adapt itself to the most solemn ritual, the most imposing services; and, therefore, the choir and sanctuary must be vast and spacious, the aisles clear for processions, the sacristies numerous and ample. We are building not for a parish, but for a whole diocese. Therefore, the space for worshippers must be very great, there must be many small chapels and oratories, and opportunity for endless tombs and tablets. We are to glorify God through art. There-

CXXI. VICTORIA CATHEDRAL. (Wilson.)

fore, the best that can be found in all the world is none too good. I shall speak of architectural style in the concluding chapter, passing the question here, only saying that the cathedral built to-day, like those built centuries ago, must grow like any of God's creatures; it must *live:* every stone must enter perfectly into the being of what is almost a sentient thing. Every shaft and arch and vault, every buttress, wall, and pinnacle, must play its just and perfect part: there must be no waste of force and no weakness, no faulty proportion, no ill-considered mass. Rheims and Amiens and Durham are crystalline, for you cannot add to them nor take away, they are rounded into perfection of life; and, as they are, so must our work be also.

These are some of the things that come down to us unchanged, and that must be demanded of architects. Of the qualities that are no longer essential, there are few; and, such as they are, they apply chiefly to administration. We no longer have monastic orders intimately connected with cathedral foundations, and there are usually lacking the resident canons who make possible constant daily service before the high altar. So the presbytery and choir need not be quite as large as in the past, though, as the result of this, the chapels must be at least equally numerous.

Of the new requirements, that of accommodating the largest number of people, with the smallest proportion of those who cannot see either the altar or the pulpit, is the most important. The inexorable law here is that this shall be considered up to the point where there would be the slightest loss architecturally, but not one step further. The chief result of this requirement is the throwing open of all the central part of the church, the abolition of the solid, monastic choir screen, and the piercing of vistas diagonally through aisles and chapels,—really, a good thing in itself, and tending to a bettering of the architectural effect.

It would not seem from this that the problem had materially changed. How could it? The Church is essentially immutable, and essentially her architectural expression must be the same. The old ideals persist and control us in our labors. Following them, we can hardly go wrong, the danger lies only in breaking recklessly away.

Latterly in England a tendency has manifested itself in this direction: the impulse toward a new vitality has rather out·

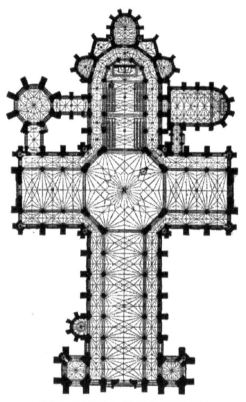

CXXII.  EXAMPLE OF BAD PLANNING.

stripped itself.   In Figure CXXI. I have shown an example of this rather exaggerated effort.   I shall speak of this again in the closing chapter.   I refer to it now simply as an example of a danger that may threaten from too wide a divergence from precedent. Brilliant as it is, original, living, and full of religious feeling, it yet lacks just that seriousness of purpose and that continuity of style that are absolutely imperative.

For, at the risk of what may seem wearisome reiteration, I must continue to insist on the necessity of preserving the continuity of architectural idea, in order that we may adequately show forth the perfect continuity of the Church. It is illogical and unjustifiable to permit ourselves to be led away into unfamiliar paths at the instigation of self-willed ecclesiastics or ambitious architects. With the classic styles we have, and can have, absolutely nothing whatever to do. Sir Christopher Wren was an episode, and St. Paul's cathedral is an episode also. It and the spirit it exemplifies were an intrusion into the Church; and, if they represent anything, they represent an occurrence that we are now endeavoring to forget.

I have referred before to the danger that once threatened of a classical cathedral in the diocese of Washington. This danger has probably passed; but, so long as it continued, every one who was interested in seeing a true architectural development of the Church in America must have trembled with apprehension. A cathedral in Washington, built in what I am, perhaps, justified in calling the " Jesuit " style of architecture, could only have set back the architectural progress of the Church to an incalculable degree. The same thing is true of the now discredited Romanesque, and as well of French Gothic. The former was, as I have said, a local and evanescent fashion: the latter, while no criticisms can be brought against it from an architectural standpoint, is nevertheless forbidden us from ethnic and historic reasons. Our succession is through the Scottish and Anglican Churches: our blood is that of Great Britain. In every possible way we are tied to England and her traditions, and whatever we do architecturally in the service of the Church must be done as a development and continuation of her history.

I have spoken frequently of the importance of the plan as the governing principle in every scheme. It was always held as such in all the great periods of the past; and the measured plan of any one of the cathedrals of the Middle Ages is almost as interesting, almost as much a work of art, as the exterior. Examine the old plans I have printed in this chapter. In every case they are masterpieces of composition, of the spacing of voids, of the proportioning of solids, and of the tracing of contours. In this very fact lies, I think, one proof of the essential greatness of the mediæval builders. Totally without architectural training, they nevertheless felt the laws of architecture so keenly that they were driven to do work which was in itself masterly.

Compare with any one of these plans that which I have shown in Figure CXXII., one of those submitted in the competition for the New York cathedral, and I think it will be recognized at once that in the modern example is a total lack of proportion, composition, and as well that "inevitable" quality that marks all the work of the Middle Ages. There is no central idea, and nothing develops from anything else. The proportions are fatal, the arrangement of chapels casual and without sufficient excuse. It may be that this question of planning is essentially one that appeals to an architect more than to a layman, but it is fundamental.

In Figure CXXIII. I have endeavored to show a scheme for such a cathedral as is usually demanded in this country. As will be seen, its basis is the typical English plan, its dominating feature is the great central tower, the point which differentiates the English from the French idea; for in the latter case the façade is the culminating point. I cannot but feel that the English type is far more architectural and possessed of greater possibilities of splendid development than the type in vogue

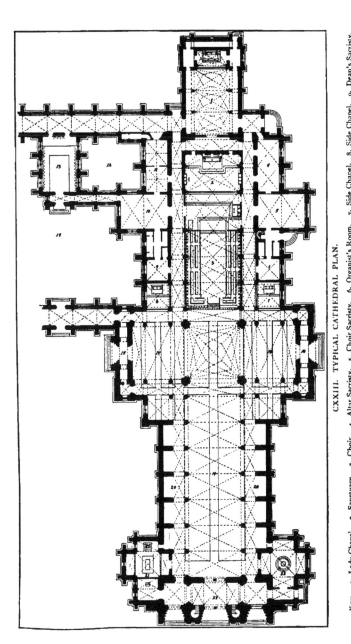

CXXIII. TYPICAL CATHEDRAL PLAN.

Key.—1. Lady Chapel. 2. Sanctuary. 3. Choir. 4. Altar Sacristy. 5. Choir Sacristy. 6. Organist's Room. 7. Side Chapel. 8. Side Chapel. 9. Dean's Sacristy. 10. Clergy's Sacristy. 11. Bishops' Sacristies. 12. Bishops' Cloister. 13. Chapter House. 14. Great Cloister. 15. North Porch. 16. South Porch. 17. North Transept. 18. South Transept. 19. Nave. 20. Chantries and Tombs. 21. Calvary and Mortuary Chapel. 22. Baptistery. 23. Narthex.

across the Channel. Also this plan provides for a double transept; that is, for a secondary transept eastward of the crossing.
This also is a particularly fine development of English composition. In deference to contemporary prejudices, the nave
is made very wide, in order that all the seats may be placed

CXXIV. VICTORIA CATHEDRAL. (Competitive design.)

within the arcades, giving a clear view of the altar from nearly
every seat. The requisite shadow is given by narrow ambulatories, which are built out into small chapels or niches for
monuments between the buttresses.

As I have said before, the great weakness of the English plan
lies in the narrowing of the church at the central point,— that
is, the crossing,— the only attempt at obviating this — namely,
the octagonal lantern of Ely — having been really a failure. I

have endeavored to obviate this effect by reducing the size of the main supports and adding subsidiary supports at the angles, also by developing these same angles so as to give that " opening out " effect I have before spoken of as being so desirable. This treatment has another advantage, in that it gives to all the seats in the transepts a clear view of the altar. Two secondary altars have been provided, opening directly into the transepts and so arranged that a large number of seats may be used when services are held at these altars. This is most desirable, for in any cathedral there will of course be many services where the high altar would scarcely be used. The English system of having small services at the high altar, the congregation occupying the stalls, cannot be condemned too vigorously; and it is a corruption against which we must carefully guard here in America.

The choir has of course been made deep and spacious, for this is absolutely necessary on certain occasions; and the cathedral must be conceived with regard to the greatest demands that will ever be made upon it. The east transept does not project in its full height to the lines of the two sacristies, but would probably extend only one narrow bay, just covering the choir ambulatory. In these transepts above the ambulatory, galleries could be provided for the orchestra and auxiliary choir of women's voices. Another great advantage of this second transept is that it makes possible great windows, which will throw desirable light directly into the sanctuary.

The Lady Chapel is given its traditional position to the eastward of the high altar. Above the reredos would be a great arched opening not filled with glass, but giving a view through to the end of the Lady Chapel. Sacristies for the bishop, dean, clergy, choir, and choirmaster, as well as the working or altar sacristy, have been arranged with due regard to convenience of administration. To the north a cloister (incomplete on the plan) has been shown; and in this cloister is the chapter house, which has direct communication also with the clergy vestry, and the bishop's sacristy. Beyond would come the various diocesan buildings, arranged as circumstances and conditions might demand.

Returning to the main front, the entrance would be through three deeply recessed porches to a large narthex, which on the north would open into a Calvary chapel, to be used also as a mortuary chapel, with a vault under. In a corresponding position on the south is the baptistery.

I have shown no exterior view of this scheme; but, to express consistently the Church in all her history, the style should be that to which I have constantly referred as the only one on which we have an unquestionable claim,— that is, the last perpendicular of the fifteenth century, the most brilliant example of which is the Chapel of Henry VII. at Westminster. The whole mass would be dominated by a great central tower, buttressed by nave, choir, and transepts. To the west the two subordinate towers would be kept low, and to the east a secondary transept would echo the support given the central tower by the towers at the west. The aisles would be practically without light, the clerestory filled with very large windows, and at the west end over the narthex and between the two towers a still larger window filling the entire space.

The scheme I have shown is arranged for masonry vaulting; and this should be employed, or at all events contemplated, in every case.

It is deeply to be desired that some opportunity may offer for the building of a great and typical cathedral in this country. If one could be constructed, or at all events begun, with a due regard to all the principles which should underlie true church-

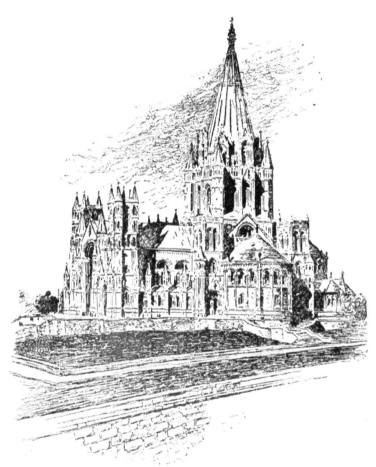

CXXV. NEW YORK CATHEDRAL (ACCEPTED DESIGN).

building, it would undoubtedly result in fixing for a century the style of ecclesiastical architecture in this country; and, once established on correct lines, we should soon see a development of ecclesiastical architecture which might easily rank with the best of that which we have had in the past.

But, if this is to occur, there must be no more trifling with a score of different styles and ideas. We must fix on a logical and consistent system of procedure. Indeed, I do not think that I am saying too much when I say that it would be well worth the cost, were the Church in America to have some convention or conference devoted exclusively to this most important question of architectural expression. I protest that it is a matter of profound importance; and, if there could be summoned to some such conference as I suggest the representative ecclesiastical architects of the country, and perhaps several from Great Britain as well, the problem could easily be settled beyond a question on sane and satisfactory lines.

# THE ARTIST CRAFTS

Nowhere are the arts more interdependent, nowhere is the major art of architecture more helpless without the intimate coöperation of every other possible art, than in the case of the Church. Here all arts meet at a common focus, and here they are called together to a common end as in no other category of activity. There are places where architecture can almost muddle through alone, places where with the aid of painting and sculpture it can thoroughly well perform its function; but in the case of a great church or cathedral the one, or even the three, are only a beginning, a foundation. We frequently forget this fact since centuries of ignorance and barbarism have despoiled our sanctuaries, thieving the treasure of gold and silver and precious stones, shattering and defacing sculpture, painting, and glass, so leaving a once living shrine a barren and whitewashed monument; and since in equal measure ignorance and barbarism have condemned the attempted restoration of what they had destroyed, denied religion its most potent agency of influence and self-expression, and substituted for a living and opulent Catholicism a dead and penurious Protestantism, — or, worse, an empty-headed agnosticism.

We have re-learned enough to enable us to venerate the isolated architecture of Amiens or Exeter, but while these and their fellows a brutal iconoclasm has not spoiled are, as pure architecture, monuments of a great and perished civilization, they are in no respect the shrines of art they once were in happier and more Christian days; then the primary art was only one of a great fellowship, and your mediæval bishop or master of works could no more have conceived of the icy emptiness of Beauvais or the echoing shell of York as a proper

CXXVI. A WINDOW.                    Charles Connick.

church than he could have conceived of the utilitarian and capitalistic organism of the nineteenth century, void of religion and of art, as a proper civilization.

In the good days of Christian society — from 1050 to 1250, — and in the crumbling and decadent days as well, on to 1550, a church was a plexus of all the arts known to man, many of which are long since forgotten. Then the architecture was, as always, the beginning; but it was far from being the end. Stone carving came to floriate shaft and cornice, pinnacle, panel, and niche; sculpture to crowd every aperture with saints and angels; painting and gilding to make all burn with radiant fire; glass-making to pierce the opaque walls and set there fields of apocalyptic glory; needlework to hang rich arras over cold stone, to clothe altars, shrines, and priests in iridescent vestments; mosaic to sheet arch and vault in burnished gold and azure and vermilion; metal work to fashion screens and candelabra of iron and bronze and brass; joinery to raise wainscot of intricate tracery; goldsmithing to furnish shrines and reliquaries and sacred vessels of precious metals and precious stones; poetry to create great hymns and canticles; drama to build up a supreme ritual; music to breathe the breath of divine life into all.

There is some difference between this, the great Christian ideal of a church and of the ministry of art, and, we will say, the later ideal of the eighteenth and nineteenth centuries, a difference that marks with some accuracy the corresponding difference between the two civilizations.

When the change came, the inevitable revolt against unendurable barbarism, it was architecture that recovered first, with music (of sorts) in second place; but all between was an aching void. Stained glass began to struggle to the light, but it was either, as in England, bound to the chariot wheels of a conserva-

John T. Comes.   Made by James T. Wolley.

CXXVII.  ALTAR BRASSES.

CXXVIII.  LOCK.

Made by Koralewsky.

tive archæleogy, or, as in America, hitched to the star of an insane anarchy. When William Morris took up the cause of the
dead arts he breathed his own superabounding vitality into the
moribund forms, and for a time they almost lived — in him —
and glass, metal work, stuffs, embroidery, tapestries came into
existence that had not been matched in the West in four centuries. All passed with his passing, however, and it was not
until a generation later that the leaven he had implanted began
working in the lump.

When this book first appeared, it is somewhat significant
that it gave only passing reference to arts other than architecture; there were no others to talk about, at least so far as the
Church was concerned. Fifteen years has shown a marvellous change, and, where then were only John Evans standing
strongly for good architectural sculpture, Irving & Casson for
honest joinery, and Heinigke & Bowen for something of the
old and living quality of stained glass, now there are one or
more brilliant and startlingly competent practitioners in every
art but one. Let me name a few of the real artists in some of
the more conspicuous categories, not to the condemnation or
exclusion of others, but to "adorn the tale" with the names of
some of those with whom I have come most in personal con-
tact during the last score of years.

In architectural sculpture there are Lee Laurie and Sterling
Calder, both capable of real sculpture on the enduring lines of
Greek and Gothic art, which are fundamentally the same; in
wood carving there is I. Kirchmayer, that amazing craftsman
out of the fifteenth century, living and thinking and working in
the twentieth century. To Heinigke & Bowen in glass have
been added younger, and as yet not wholly tried men — Connick,
d'Ascenzo, Young — who are all working backward toward a
recovery of the old and eternal laws and methods of the most

Made by Gebelein.

CXXIX. PROCESSIONAL CROSS.

finally perfected art of man, the glass of the thirteenth century. For goldsmiths and workers in the finer metals we have Hunt, Wooley, Gebelein, who have of late made crosses and candlesticks, chalices and reliquaries that meet and match the work of the Middle Ages on its own grounds. The iron work of Yellen, and of Krasser (lately dead, alas, but fortunately leaving behind him an established tradition that will continue at the hands of the craftsmen he has trained, chiefest of whom is Koralewsky) is well of the sort that would have made them blood brothers of Adam Kraft. In the making of wonderful tiles of vivid designs and strange glazes we have Miss Perry, and Mercer and Dulles-Allen; in altar needlework, Miss Barton; in illumination, Friedley, Dean, Mountfort-Smith; in heraldry, LaRose; while Herter and Baumgarten have gone far toward restoring to life the glorious art of tapestry weaving.

It is a surprising and an inspiring list, the more so in that it is practically the emanation of the last fifteen years, and in the fact that this astonishing growth of Christian artist-crafts has taken place lies the greatest encouragement for genuine religious art that has shown itself in that period. No notable development in ecclesiastical architecture has occurred in the same space of time, (though fine work has been done both in Great Britain and America;) but this was hardly to be expected. The sound and enduring and very simple old principles of church building had already been established, and it was, and is, merely a question of the slow acceptance of these by parsons and architects and people in place of the false ideas that had grown up during four centuries, and of the equally slow development of men who could carry them out in loyalty and reverence and sincerity. With the artist-crafts, however, it was quite a different matter: here there were no leaders, no

CXXX. FOUR STATUES. I. Kirschmayer.

guides, no teachers; there was not even a general demand, for every one seemed perfectly content with the wares of the "Ecclesiastical Decorator and Furnisher." Yet the thing has come to pass, and in the most natural and wholesome way, for without any incisive or stimulating propaganda, without anything approaching concerted action, true craftsmen have risen up to sustain the hands of the architect, and to give to the Church the art she needed for her perfect expression.

As for the causes that have led up to this most desirable result, it is hard to assign them with any definiteness. The widespread " Arts and Crafts " movement has had something to do with it undoubtedly, at least in its beginnings. Many of those I have named are either members of some local organization or inspired by its activity, but there can be less connection now than in the past, since this same movement has abandoned, in so many cases, its fundamental principle, which was that the man who designed should execute, the man who executed should design. This must be the unflinching law of all good artist-craftmanship, and it holds most tenaciously in the case of ecclesiastical art. Probably one great agent has been the growing revolt against an insane capitalism by reason of the dawning consciousness that its inevitable result, if not its aim, was a new and awful slavery, and against that commercialism in art which has already destroyed the art if it has crowned the commerce with success. All the good work of which I have spoken is done by individual craftsmen, mostly poor, universally independent — a great and triumphant advance over the appalling conditions of a generation ago. Compared with the highly organized capitalistic basis of this sort of thing, the new independence and individuality is economically sound, and therefore fruitful of good art, but it can never reach its full efficiency until recourse is had to the old guild system of the Middle

Font made by John Evans.     Cover by H. Wilson, England.
CXXXI.  ST. JAMES' CHURCH, ROXBURY, MASS.

Ages, which is the only righteous and economically decent basis of production. Finally, there has been a psychological, if not a clearly expressed material, demand, and this has, of course, resulted in a certain supply. Even in the midst of the dull acceptance of the wares of commercial purveyors there has been, deep down underneath the surface, a vague hungering for something better, something approximating more nearly the products of the Christian ages of civilization, and the artist-craftsmen *in posse* have heard and have answered.

Considering the brief space allowed for development since this restoration began, the products in many categories are of a singularly and even startlingly high order. Kirchmayer's wood carving, whether in figure sculpture, or decorative work, is full of a keen personality, that emphasizes rather than negatives its underlying qualities of sound tradition and good art; it is Mediæval as the new Gothic is trying to be Mediæval — such in spirit and in suggestion, but at the same time contemporary and without archæological affectation. His best work is done when he is given a free hand, without full-sized drawings or even sketches, and then, without the intervention of models or even drawings of his own, he proceeds to cut from some baulk of solid oak a figure of saint or angel inspired with the very spirit of that art of the Middle Ages that is so comprehensive and vital that it is of all time rather than of any given epoch.

The same is true of Krasser, Yellen, Koralewski, in the domain of iron-forging, and some of their work has the life and spirit, the vivid beauty and the masterly craftsmanship of the best of the ironwork of the XVth and XVIth centuries.

If the workers in brass and copper have not as yet quite reached the originality and power in independent design of Kirchmayer or Krasser, they fall no degree behind them in tech-

CXXXII. ALTAR, CHRIST CHURCH, MALDEN.

Made by Irving & Casson.

nical mastery, and of late work has been produced, that in touch and texture is consummate in its perfection.

Already Miss Perry's tiles are famous, with their wonderful glazes that recall the triumphs of the great potters of the Ming dynasty, while the amazingly original and captivating designs that Mercer produces at Doylestown have achieved a place, in the estimation of those who know, that is unique and unchallenged.

I might go on through all the other categories of the artist-crafts, noting the almost incredible restoration of fifteen years; but it would be simply a repetition of the same adjectives. In every case there seems to be independent action toward a new art that — being good art — is also old, and now, instead of architecture reaching back to help along these allied arts without whose aid its labour is half in vain, it is now a case of architecture looking out for the varied arts that follow close to heel and being compelled to take care lest it is overtaken and passed by those rivals that once were humble followers.

Two points may be noted in what I have said of the new artist-crafts, and the first is the scant sprinkling of American or English names amongst those unmistakably of foreign lineage; the second that painting is not included amongst the resurgent arts. The prominence of Teutonic names is due in part to the fact that overseas there has been by no means so complete a débâcle and collapse of craftsmanship as here, or even in Great Britain. In this country, by the middle of the last century, even the tradition of true handicraft had died away, while by the beginning of the present century even the trades had practically ceased to be anything but the clumsy and perfunctory following of stolid conventions bad enough in themselves. This latter process of degeneration has continued unchecked until, at the present time, the labour unions have

J. Kirschmayer.

CXXXIII.  ST. ANTHONY OF PADUA.

succeeded in reducing all the trades they direct and control to a dead level of inefficiency. Recently on one piece of work alone, where only men of good standing were employed, I had to take off my coat, get hold of the necessary tools, and actually show the men how to tool stone, point masonry joints, plaster a wall, finish ironwork, and give the right texture, colour, and surfacing to joinery, while on the same job, where there was much elaborate woodcarving, the contractor (highly recommended as a first-class man) sent all his Gothic carving to the works, put it in place, and finished it, just as it came from the machine carver, without the touch of a hand chisel. The workmen knew no better; they wanted to do the right kind of thing, but they had no training, and the unions had abolished in them all pride in mastery, all ambition to excel. To the purveyor of machine-made carving this was the only kind there was, and he was inordinately proud of his clever and expeditious machines. The tradition was gone, however, the tradition of getting the best and knowing how to get it; and in Germany, in France to a certain extent, and here and there in Great Britain, this same tradition still persists, though in a vanishing degree.

And the United States, and the states, and the cities, with all their elaborate educational activities, do nothing either to arrest this decay or to help their own citizens to become skilled workmen and meet the demand that is now being supplied by aliens. France maintains at public expense innumerable schools for the training of craftsmen of many sorts, and Germany does the same; but in America, where the clamour for "vocational training" is at its height, it is apparently held that this is accomplished by the furnishing of schools for the teaching of bookkeeping, stenography, business administration, and journalism; that wood carving and stone

CXXXIV.  A ROMAN CATHOLIC CHANCEL.    John T. Comes, Architect.

carving and fine metal work and stained glass and joinery are also " vocational " subjects does not seem to suggest itself to the astute minds of professional educators.   Therefore the American citizen becomes a common labourer, while the high crafts and the well paid are turned over to the skilled immigrants from Germany and Scandinavia, Poland and France.   The architect has little cause, therefore, to thank the Government of America, but great cause to be grateful to the Governments of France and Germany and the rest of Europe, which in this respect at least show superior intelligence and immeasurably greater generosity.

As for painting, the question at once arises why, with the advance in the other arts subsidiary to architecture, there has thus far been here no corresponding advance.   England, Germany, and Scandinavia have all produced during the last fifty years monumental and decorative painters of right impulse and great ability ; even France, with a wholly wrong principle at the bottom of its system of training, and with a malignant hatred of religion in every form throned in high places, has not been without great men.   Here in America no single painter has as yet come forward to paint for the Church as his forbears of centuries ago painted for the Church and gloried in (and existed by) the act.   I am not speaking of secular painting for monumental and decorative purposes.   Here we have men of eminence and accomplishment ; but in the domain of religious painting there is no one to whom the architect or the donor can turn for altar-piece, shrine, votive picture, or wall painting.   This is partly due to the fact that most of the trained men are born and bred in the ateliers of the Ecole des Beaux-Arts (where the religious picture is either an impertinence or an empty academic exercise), and partly to the most curious fact that amongst these painters, from whom (judged

B. G. Goodhue, Architect.

CXXXV. BALTIMORE CATHEDRAL.

by their secular work) one had good ground for hoping for something real in religious art, there is either the cool indifferentism to religion, or the scornful contempt born of irreligious inheritance, environment, and education, or a wandering off after strange heresies or novel orientalisms, equally born of, though this time as reactions from, the same irreligious inheritance, environment, and education.

Now so long as this is true there will be no great, or even passable painters of religious art. The carver, or iron-worker, or glass-maker may, without faith, yet achieve a measure of craft capacity, at all events enough to set him far before his untrained and careless fellows; but in painting the case is quite different. It is the mysteries of the Catholic Faith that reveal themselves through the brush of the painter, so handled as to be a channel of inspiration and of revelation; the mysteries of the Annunciation and the Nativity, the Crucifixion and the Resurrection; the mysteries of angels and archangels, cherubim and seraphim, prophets and martyrs and confessors; the mysteries of the Sacraments and the Communion of Saints, of the Rosary and of the Sacred Heart; the mysteries that transcend reason, negative the intellect, form the heart and the crown of religion, and reveal themselves only, in symbolical form, through painting and music, poetry and sculpture and architecture.

From the Unitarian you may not expect a painted revelation of the Mystery of the Incarnation; from a Christian Scientist the Mystery of the Passion of Christ; from a Presbyterian the Mystery of the Mother of Mercy, " Our Lady of Pity; " from a follower of some Indian Swami the Mystery of the Seven Sacraments. From each might come great art of other kinds, but not this, the art of Catholic Christianity; and so long as it is Catholic Christianity that clamours loudest for

Sir Robert Lorimer, Architect.

CXXXVI. STALLS IN THE THISTLE CHAPEL, EDINBURGH.

the ministry of art, so long must the Catholic Church wait for the Catholic painter who from devotion and not from ambition, from humility and not from technical proficiency, will paint again for her, as Cimabue painted, and Giotto; Fra Angelico, Memeling, Van Eyck, Luini, da Vinci, and Tintoretto.

# A RETROSPECT

As has been indicated in the last chapter, the developments in ecclesiastical art during the last fifteen years have been more notable in the domain of the allied arts than in architecture itself. There the change has been one wholly of quality, — the real taking the place of the false, — here it is one only of degree. This is inevitable, for fifteen years ago the great fight that began with the Pugins for the restoration to the Church of her own native and personal art, and was given a reason for being and a power of achievement by the Oxford Movement, which aimed at the restoration to Ecclesia Anglicana of her Catholic heritage, had already been won in England, and in fact even in America, though here the visible fruits were less conspicuous. The various cults and fads of church building had already been discredited, and everywhere the attempt was being made to regain control of the Gothic or Christian style in some form or other, whenever a church was to be built.

Since then the process of restoration has gone on without a pause; it is safe to say that, within the last five years, practically all the church work has been Gothic both by intention and effect. The Protestant denominations have been behindhand in no respect, and they press their Episcopalian fellows hard in their career of building towering, great Gothic structures that might deceive the very elect into thinking that within they would find the doctrine, discipline, and ritual of Catholicity. Thanks largely to two strikingly able men, — Mr. Maginnis and Mr. Comes, — the Roman Catholic Church has been in a measure won away from her well-established course of building architectural aberrations, and now one fre-

CXXXVIII. ST. THOMAS' CHURCH, NEW YORK.

quently finds perfect models of good Gothic art rising under her direction.

In the light of the really great revolution accomplished in the last decade, the arguments and prayers for the acceptance of sound principles and beautiful forms in church building, as these appear in the first chapters of this book, will, to new readers, seem inexplicable in their intensity; for if ever there was an overwhelming victory it is this particular battle for sound Christian architecture. Fifteen years ago, however, the issue was far less undebatable, and there were few then, and particularly the author of this book, who would have dared to predict a triumph so eminent and so complete.

There is, therefore, little to record in the way of novelty; the conviction has steadily grown that honesty of construction is as imperative as good style, both from a theological and an æsthetic standpoint, and such deplorable expedients as that referred to on page 84 would now be hardly conceivable, outside the limits of the Roman Catholic Church, which is still under the heavy cloud of artistic subterfuge. Again there is an increasing consciousness that neither ornaments, nor " picturesqueness," nor ecclesiastical accuracy have as much to do with real Gothic as have form and mass and composition and light and shade, and that finally, whatever else it is, a good church must be absolutely organic, a living thing in impulse, form, and structure.

Of course the output of churches in fifteen years has been enormous, and a large proportion of these are probably destined to be enduring monuments. In America, when this book was first published, while there were many small churches of charm and merit, there were comparatively few of great size couched in the terms of Gothic well understood ; now there are many, and not alone of the Episcopal Church, which never

CXXXIX. CALVARY CHURCH, PITTSBURGH.

had wholly lost the tradition of great religious art, but notably
of those denominations whose beginnings were complicated
with an eager hatred of art of any kind. That the Episcopal
Church should build such structures as St. Thomas', New York,
or Calvary, Pittsburgh, was to be expected; it would have been
shameful if she had not; but it was perhaps hardly to be fore-
seen that the Baptists would have taken kindly and instinctively
to their Pittsburgh church, or that the Presbyterians would have
eagerly welcomed their new structures in Chicago, Cleveland
and St. Paul. But they did, and in this fact lies, I think, one
of the very great encouragements, not only in church building
but in religion as well.

With the Roman Catholics, while there have been such
notable contributions to Gothic art as Mr. Maginnis' fine parish
churches and Mr. Comes' equally noble structure, there has been
also a new development of that little known Lombard type the
former handles so perfectly. This is a style of great purity,
mobility, and charm. Only a great artist can cope with it adequately, for it is subtle and baffling to a degree, and it forms
the only conceivable rival for the normal Gothic of the
Catholic Church.

In looking over the foregoing chapter on " The Cathedral "
it is rather pathetic to note the straits to which one was drawn
to find illustrations of contemporary work. Albany, Truro,
Belfast, and Cleveland, with a few problematical architectural
designs, was literally all there was for the Anglican communion
in England and America, while for the Roman Church in the
same lands St. Patrick's in New York was really about all there
was, except Westminster, London, then not ready for occu-
pancy. Now it is a question not of searching but of choosing.
Rome has Westminster as an accomplished fact, as glorious
and awe-inspiring within as it is ineffective without; in simple

CXL. FOURTH PRESBYTERIAN CHURCH, CHICAGO.

fact the greatest interior since the fifteenth century. It also has the pure and scholarly monument in Norwich; and in America, St. Louis, St. Paul, and Pittsburgh. In England the "Establishment" is slowly rearing that masterly vision of living beauty, Liverpool. In America the allied Church is building on and around the first fragment in New York, chapels, schools, a bishop's palace, a deanery, and a great synod hall; in Detroit is a true cathedral lacking structurally only its central tower; in Washington beginnings have been made on a vast structure that will fix forever in history the names of Bodley and of Vaughan; San Francisco is rearing its metropolitan church on the flame-swept heights, while Baltimore has adopted Mr. Goodhue's vision of a great and glorious church and moves slowly toward its accomplishment in space and time; finally, in Canada, Halifax is approaching completion, while Toronto has just been begun.

It is rather an inspiring record of fifteen years, showing not alone the vitality of the Church, but the power of the cathedral idea and the direct appeal it makes to the world after so many centuries when cathedrals were destroyed instead of edified, and even the Church itself was marked by man for immediate destruction, or a more prolonged, but no less definite, decay.

Stylistically the record is one of a generally high order of design and integrity of construction. The three great English cathedrals are sufficiently diverse in type and handling; but all are marked by splendid impulse and consummate mastery. The cathedral at Westminster is the result of the proximity of the great Abbey church that made rivalry impossible; therefore the architect, much against his will, was denied his instinctive Gothic and forced to work in, to him, an alien style. That it was such would not be suspected from the result, for Westmin-

CXLI.  DETROIT CATHEDRAL.

ster cathedral is one of the few really great architectural con-
ceptions of modern times. What Bentley could have done in
Gothic is shown by his exquisite and faultless little Church of
the Holy Rood, Watford, and looking at this one is tempted to
regret the chance that drove him to Byzantium for his London
inspiration. Once within Westminster walls, however, the regret vanishes, and one is thankful that the exigencies of the
situation made possible this sublime temple, proved that great
architects can exist in the modern ages, and demonstrated that
after all styles count less than the world had thought ; that the
everlasting modes of the past are at one in all essentials, and
that what really counts is genius surcharged with a radiant and
living Christian faith.

Norwich is far at the other diameter of the circle of
styles, for it is of a severe and formal and scholarly thirteenth-
century Gothic ; very competent, very erudite, a Catholic
church of the enduring Catholic type. Liverpool again is
asunder from both, for it is as far removed from precedent
as possible. It is, perhaps, the most alive of all modern
churches, the work of a man who lives and breathes in the
very spirit of the Middle Ages, and so much so that precedent
is as little to him as it was to the creator of the west front of
Paris or the chevêt of Le Mans. After Liverpool he looks
very foolish who says that Gothic is a dead style and cannot
be made to live again. Judging from the Lady Chapel, the
only portion at present completed, Liverpool will take its
place with Chartres and Lincoln and Seville as one of the
great manifestations of a great and deathless style. Some
of us balk a little at the wild and mystical ornament, preferring
ever our Hugh of St. Victor to our St. Bonaventure, and
regret as well the violent change that has been made in the
church itself, whereby its long and simple nave becomes a

Maginnis & Walsh, Architects.

CXLII. A ROMAN CATHOLIC CHURCH, SOMERVILLE, MASS.

vast basilica, and its original and most novel transeptal towers are lost forever; but after all the man who could create the Lady Chapel cannot possibly go very wrong, and with full confidence in Mr. Scott, — the third in direct succession of a wonderful line of master-builders, — we wait patiently the issue of his labours, confident that this will involve no shadow of disappointment.

In America nothing yet has arisen to rival Liverpool either in size or splendour, though several wonders are in the making. Mr. Bodley's Washington is now in the hands of Mr. Vaughan, and gives promise in time of being one of those masterly monuments of scholarly perfection, — a recreation of the fourteenth century in the twentieth, — that one safely counts on from the present architect as one did from his predecessor. What San Francisco is to prove one is not as yet quite sure. Here again, originally, recourse was had to Bodley, as at Washington, in preference to any American architect; but his death brought the first plans to an end and everything is now in the hands of local men. Planned originally for a site impossible both in point of its restricted area and its unearthly topography, Bodley almost won victory out of defeat and produced a striking scheme that bade defiance to all limitations. The old site is still retained with all its imperfections on its head, but the first design is wholly abandoned and it is too soon to predict what its successor will prove. Detroit is unmistakably a cathedral in spite of its comparatively small dimensions, and is an example of how much can be done when land and funds are both restricted. It is of an easy and adaptable type of Gothic, as is Baltimore, which is of cathedral proportions as well as design, — a mobile, poetic, almost dramatic design as now conceived, and far and away the most consistent and promising of

Gilbert Scott, Architect.

CXLIII. LADY CHAPEL, LIVERPOOL CATHEDRAL.

I. Kirschmayer, Carver.

CXLIV.  LADY ALTAR AND TRIPTYCH.

all the American cathedral schemes which have been conceived *de novo*. What will happen at the Cathedral of St. John the Divine in New York is at present uncertain. The original scheme has been abandoned by the trustees, and a new and completed plan worked out under the direction of the present consulting architect; and meanwhile subsidiary structures are rising all around the original fragment, — a synod hall, choir school, bishop's palace, and deanery, while no less than five chapels are being added to (and completing) the chevêt. This is all being done by different architects, — Vaughan, Walter Cook, Carrere & Hastings and Cram, Goodhue & Ferguson, — for after the expiration of the contract with the architects of the choir the trustees tried the experiment of dividing the work amongst several firms, with a consulting architect at the head. All but one chapel are explicitly Gothic in style, with transitional French leanings so far as palace, deanery, synod hall, and one chapel are concerned, English fourteenth century for three of the other chapels, and fifteenth century for the choir school. The remaining chapel is of a delicate Italian early Renaissance cast, and in spite of diversity of impulse and of authorship it all holds together suprisingly well. The consulting architect took the position that if the trustees wanted to employ different architects of pronounced individuality, he himself could be no party to the coercion of any of them into working in a style or after a fashion with which he had no sympathy. He therefore contented himself with establishing certain restrictions as to the mass and scale of the chevêt chapels, so that these, as already determined by Heins & LaFarge, might be strictly adhered to, and with preserving an essential unity, or harmony of material, and then each architect was free to work out his best ideas after his own best fashion.

CXLV. TENTATIVE SCHEME FOR THE CATHEDRAL OF ST. JOHN THE DIVINE,
NEW YORK.

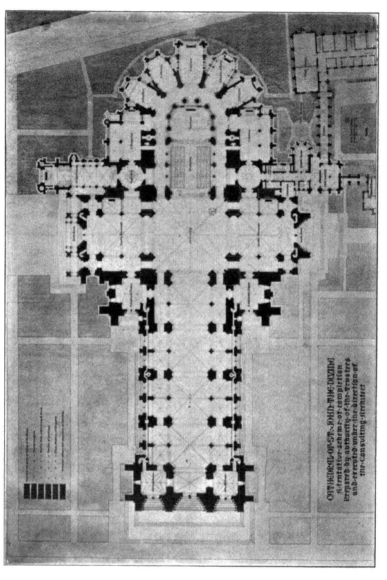

CXLVI.  PLAN OF THE CATHEDRAL OF ST. JOHN THE DIVINE, NEW YORK.

Ideal as this plan may seem in theory, and feasible as it would have been at any time in the past, it is questionable if it can safely be adhered to now, since there is no such thing as a consistent impulse behind the practice of architecture, or anything approaching stylistic unity. In the thirteenth century religion was one, and society, and art, and the difference between, for example, William of Sens and William the Englishman, at Canterbury, was a difference only in detail. Behind both was the same driving force, the same faith, the same artistic impulse, so one could easily continue what the other had initiated, without any resulting jar or discrepancy. These conditions no longer exist, and, where one building has several architects in succession, it can only show drastic and even startling variations, for every man is feeling his way, through experiment and error, it may be, toward an ultimate fixed basis still wholly obscured.

Is this distant goal of unity, of a " national style, " any nearer after fifteen years; is its nature more clearly to be discovered? Honesty answers in the negative. If anything, there are more kinds of style in vogue today than then: astounding fruit of miscegenation, that is yet in many ways beautiful and vital, as that of the Pacific Coast, where elements from Norway, Switzerland, Japan, and Bhutan mingle in a strange and unearthly fashion — and justify themselves in the mingling; rectilinear rigidities from the middle west (cubist even) that suggest the new stagecraft of the emancipated Teuton; Dalmatia, Venice, Byzantium, and Lombardy fused into coherence on the plains of Texas; and with them all the respectable old styles of the orderly past. The perfect chaos of society, the mingling of myriad races and traditions, the anarchy of industry, the muddleheadness of theology, the breakdown of the nineteenth-century educational system, the general aimlessness and un-

CXLVII. "SOUTH CHURCH" (DUTCH REFORMED), NEW YORK.

certainty of things react inevitably on art, and the Tower of Babel has its Babylonian showing forth in architecture.

It is evident that art cannot coördinate society; society must coördinate art, and, as it shows at present not the faintest tendency toward its own coördination, the day of a "national style" is evidently a long way off. In the meantime, since this same society has broken up almost completely into its component parts, with a resulting confusion matched only at every five-hundred year interval since the fall of Hellenic civilization (and farther back still, I dare say), it remains only for architecture to express each fragment, as best it can, whatever may be the stylistic presumption involved. This is precisely what it is doing, and doing very well indeed. We already have a perfectly definited "State House Style," and clear and plausible styles for post offices, Carnegie Libraries, metropolitan hotels, and city banks — all quite different and most of them lucid and convincing. We also have a good and consistent style for Episcopal churches, and two perfectly good styles for colleges. Probably the same process will continue indefinitely, until every field of activity develops its own logical form of artistic expression, until yellow journalism has its own manifestation, and Christian Science; equal suffrage, the moving-picture show, "big business," and the I. W. W.

Some day the process of dissolution will cease, the disintegrated atoms will again begin to coalesce, folly will be squeezed out in the process, and sanity and righteousness will resume their reign. There are evidences that this Apocalyptic moment is not so far away as contemporary conditions would argue; already there are signs of change and portents of redemption; the stupid and moribund conventions that do duty as principles, and have so served for four centuries, are losing something of their wide acceptance. Here and there strange people are

CXLVIII. THE CHAPEL AT WEST POINT.

questioning whether capitalism and industrialism are really benefits after all; why intellectualism and the "scientific method" should have aquired the absurd position they now occupy; if Protestantism is indeed an improvement over Catholicism, as some have held; if the new philosophy of Bergson (which is merely as old as St. Thomas, Plotinus, St. Augustine, and Plato) is not in fact a complete refutation of all the philosophy of the last hundred years; wherein democracy and universal suffrage and the parliamentary system have succeeded when other systems are held to have failed.   And this same scrutiny is being meted out to the hasty reforms that have offered themselves, — direct legislation, socialism, direct action, rationalism, woman suffrage, impressionism, Christian Science, — with results that hardly fortify their cases.   On the other hand, curious new events are coming to pass: men are turning to the Middle Ages for light and inspiration; the guild system comes to the front and finds such passionate defenders as Hilaire Belloc and his following; Bergson clears the way for the new disciples of St. Thomas and Hugo of St. Victor; Chesterton bursts on an astonished world; a Catholic reaction shows itself, and once more monasticism rises into sudden new life.

It is all very suprising, very stimulating, and out of it all one idea comes clearly.   No longer must the artist play his rather unnatural part of leader and prophet.   As "a voice crying in the wilderness" he may now die away, for the errors that had manifestation through the barbarism and the bad art he fought to the death are themselves now dying, and out of their fall, — over it, and because of it, — is rising a new spirit of synthesis and coördination, of life and of dynamic force; and in a few years, when the ugly and tragical process of ground-clearing has been accomplished and the new era begins its course, then the artist will revert to his just and proper position as a chan-

nel and a mouthpiece; through him will flood into visible being
in art all the life and the unity and the splendour of a new day,
and no longer will some men be forced to speculate as to the
coming of a "national style," and others to publish books on
"Church Building."

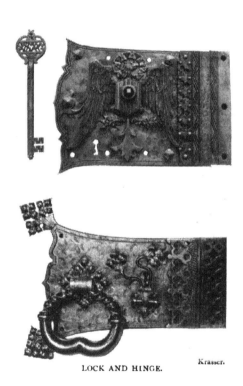

LOCK AND HINGE.

Krasser.

# CONCLUSION

In the foregoing chapters I have endeavored to formulate the idea of the church as an architectural entity, to show that church building is not simply an ordinary proposition in architectural design, but rather a problem governed by higher principles and more enduring laws than obtain in any other form of the great art of building. I have tried to indicate the difference between the modern problems of civil architecture and ecclesiastical; to show that, while in the former fashion, individual taste and temporary and changing conditions may justly be taken into account, in the latter we are confronted by a power demanding material expression, that in all essential things is unchanged and unchangeable. This fact has been forgotten for several centuries; and the result has been not only chaotic and misleading, but as well actually detrimental to the position and influence of the Church herself. For we cannot look on architecture, or on art in any of its forms, as an accidental thing, as a matter with which the Church has little concern. We must learn the lesson, once well known, but long forgotten, that art is one of the most accurate indices of civilization known to history, that it is an actual and vital power competent to do God's work through His Church surely and lastingly, and that indifference to its work or carelessness means actual and measurable loss.

By regarding her architectural and artistic expression as a matter of indifference, by leaving the subject in the hands of incompetent committees and untrained and unsympathetic architects, by following after the evanescent will-o'-the-wisps of fantastic fashion, by building, in a word, bad churches instead of good ones, as she has done for these many centuries, the Church has not only cast aside a great teaching agency, she has as well been false to a trust; for she has always been the inspiration of art, and its protector, and, when civil life fell to a level where it was no longer able to incite to artistic activity, the responsibility of the Church was doubled, for she remained then the only vital power that could insure the continuity of the artistic life of men.

It is, of course, worse than useless to mourn over what is accomplished, but we may at least consider it, in order that we may see clearly how we are to try for better things; and, in doing so, we must first realize how bad has been the work of the past three hundred years. Once admit this, and it is enough: we can then pass to the more important consideration of ways and means for effecting the reform.

The trouble has been that, from the time of Henry VIII., the Church has allowed the civil power to lead, in all matters of art, at least. This was not a safe leadership, for society was not of a nature that made possible artistic development in the line of an advance. The first impulse of the Italian Renaissance was thoroughly assimilated by England, and the Christian style made more sensitive and beautiful thereby, as may be seen by a reference to the Chapel of Henry VII. at Westminster; but, though for the moment it looked as though English Gothic was about to develop for the first time into a purely national and uniquely beautiful style, the hope was vain, and rushing political events brought collapse and catastrophe. The evolution of the great national style was cut as by a knife; and German influence under Elizabeth, debased Italian under the last of the Stuarts, and crude Dutch under the imported Hanoverians, were only stages in a constantly accelerating fall. At the beginning of the nineteenth century the deplorable progress was stayed, simply because there was no pit of farther fall.

# CONCLUSION

And always the Church had taken whatever was popular in civil life. Of course, no churches were built under Elizabeth; for there were already too many, and they could be given away to courtiers. The same was true under the first two Stuarts, though Charles I. did indeed do his best to stay the ignominious progress and effect a reaction in favor of the national and Christian Gothic. Once more a healthy movement was crushed by revolution, and with the Restoration the classical Renaissance resumed its progress. Wren, Inigo Jones, Gibbs, and their ilk were technically able men, but they were hampered by an absurd style; and they could not build churches, though they did. With them everything stopped, and for a century and a half religious architecture was non-existent. What our ancestors did in America was only crude imitation, without any artistic value whatever, and precious only from an historical standpoint. The French Revolution and its American advocate, Thomas Jefferson, brought in a further modification in the line of still greater depravity and artificiality; and here the collapse might almost seem to have stopped, for the next phase was the first flush of the great Gothic Restoration. Unfortunately, however, this was with us only an episode, though the work done by its great advocates, Upjohn and Renwick, deserved better things. But as in England, so here. There the Pugins, with their sensitive appreciation of architecture as a living thing, had been succeeded by the masters of archæology, Scott, Street, and Pierson; and the Gothic revival went backward. Here Upjohn gave place to the practitioners of "Victorian Gothic," and dryness and artificiality were the result. The Centennial was the signal for the complete break-up of all consistent building; and the deplorable chaos that followed was lightened only by the fast strengthening influence of Richardson, with his enormous vitality, his splendid sincerity and honesty. But his was an alien style, with no historic or ethnic propriety: its virtue was the virtue of its advocate alone; and with his death the fatal weakness of Romanesque became apparent. There was none to carry on the master's work. It degenerated into the most shocking barbarism, and passed into history as an episode. Yet, even if this was its lamentable fate, the greater quality of Richardson persisted; and, until French Renaissance came as the latest and freshest fad, something of honesty and directness was demanded in architecture.

In the mean time the steady and noble work of Bodley and Garner and Sedding had borne fruit in England. Victorian Gothic was suppressed, and continuity was restored with the original movement begun by Pugin. A score of brilliant men took up the task of the restoration and established it firmly; while Mr. Henry Vaughn came to America as the apostle of the new dispensation, and a few men have seized enthusiastically upon the principles he so modestly showed in his work.

Since then there has been a new development in England, and, I think, hardly a healthy one; that, namely, toward an exaggeration of the elements of originality in Sedding's work to the exclusion of those conservative qualities on which it was based. Yet I am sure that this is only a temporary phase of development, and in it is something of encouragement, though for the time it is exaggerated; for, however radical and revolutionary it may be, it is vital and contemporary, and shows how fully the younger men appreciate the necessity of making ecclesiastical architecture living, mobile, and spontaneous.

Such, briefly, is an outline of the vicissitudes of architecture since the time of Henry VIII., when its natural process of development was stopped. It is a record of confusion, of artificiality, of a complete lack of consistency and of governing motives. That it represents accurately enough the progress of general civilization may be true, as I have said in the Introduction; but that it adequately expresses the immutable Church is not true, even if we admit, as we may, that it voices her superficial, and for these hundred years her apparent, nature. We can no longer plead ignorance, lack of knowledge of the importance of art in the service of the Church, want of guidance on the part of architects toward a true and logical architectural expression. If the Church continues to show herself through flippant and fantastic styles, if she still prefers confusion and disorder and artistic failure, then she does so with a clear knowledge of what she is doing.

But that she will follow this false and unworthy course I do not believe; for she is daily growing more united, more clear-sighted, more conscious of her unity, of her position as an integral portion of the one Catholic Church, and this very consciousness must of necessity explain itself in a corresponding consistency of outward appearance.

What, then, is her duty? what is the attitude that she must maintain toward art and her own architectural expression?

First of all, she must realize that architecture is in no manner a matter of fashion, of predilection, of personal or individual tastes; that a style is good if it expresses the spiritual idea of the power that employs it, the genealogy and the history, the continuity of blood, the ethnic affiliations, and the temper of a people. Then she must understand that a chaos of styles is unendurable, and that one, and one only, can be employed at any given time. As she is one, so must her art be, also; though, once established, it may develop and expand to any degree, until it has progressed far beyond the original point of departure. Also, she must know this: that a style cannot be called out of nothingness into being, but that it must be a continuation, a development, reaching back through the ages to the very beginning of all.

# CHURCH BUILDING

In the architecture of the last three hundred years there has been neither consistency nor continuity: it is a riot of episodes,— no more.  The French Renaissance of the boulevards, rampant in secular affairs just now; Richardsonian Romanesque, only just passed into history; the jabbering argots of the quarter of a century following the Civil War, Victorian Gothic, pseudo-Gothic, Jeffersonian, Colonial, Georgian, Queen Anne, Jacobean, Elizabethan, — all are but fantastic episodes, without value except as a stern reminder of the episodical nature of the progress of post-reformation civilization.  Step by step we go back through the labyrinth of artificiality, until in Jacobean we find a certain quality of spontaneity, in Elizabethan a little more, and then, at a step, we pass from confusion to order, from posing to healthy activity, from self-consciousness to frank simplicity, from disorder to the reign of law.

For, from the coming of William the Conqueror to the death of Cardinal Wolsey, the development of Christian architecture in England had been slow, sure, and logical,— from the Norman of Durham, through the Early English of Ely and Wells, the Decorated of Canterbury and York, down to the day when William of Wykeham, bishop of Winchester, by what almost seemed divine inspiration, saw before him the next and greatest step, took it, and in a breath turned the gropings that had been hitherto into clear seeing, and so made possible the development of a form of Gothic that was at once worthy to stand with that of France, and, as well, purely and consistently English.  It is at this point that at last we are able to take up the thread of development, and not before; for, as I have said, all since was but a babel of tongues.  Before had been the constant struggle for national expression; but it was through means always a little more highly perfected across the Channel. English Gothic was always differentiated; but, until William of

Wykeham, it had fallen a little short of the wonderful products of the Christian style in France. Winchester cathedral, as it was recast by the great bishop, showed that this reproach need no longer be endured.

English Gothic had attained its majority, and from now could only be triumphant growth and advance. And such was really the case. The perfected style came into universal use, and its beauty fell like a garment over the stern old Norman and Early English cathedrals and abbeys. Unfortunately, none of these dates wholly from this time; but in Winchester, Gloucester, and Sherborne, in the Lady chapels, chantries, tombs, and reredoses of an hundred foundations, in the colleges and chapels of Oxford and Cambridge, we can see how delicate, mobile, and withal, national, was the wonderful thing William of Wykeham had brought into existence. It was logical in construction, rational, and scientific; it adapted itself to conditions as did no other phase of Gothic; it was, and is, absolutely modern, yet it was expressed through the highest forms of sensitive beauty; and, above all, it was national. It was not French, either of the Norman type of Durham or of the Geometric of Westminster. It was of England, English; and it voiced the highest qualities of the loftiest civilization,— that of the end of the fourteenth and the beginning of the fifteenth centuries.

There seems no limit to the possibilities of its growth; and yet, before it had had time to create a single consistent and complete cathedral or abbey, at the very opening of its career, it was crushed, broken, utterly swept away, and in its place came the crude and pagan classic of Wren and Inigo Jones.

Here is our starting-point. We may pass over the various fashionable styles with hardly a word, for none will be found bold enough to advocate classic architecture in any of its forms for the service of the Church. Romanesque has wrought its own downfall, and there is none so mean as to do it reverence. To Gothic we return inevitably; but the process of exclusion does not cease here. Were we to continue as now, building essays in archæology, to-day in French Flamboyant, to-morrow in Early English, here in Decorated, there in François premier, we should still be following out the old principle of artificiality. One style, and one only, is for us; and that is the English Perpendicular.

Every other phase of Gothic rose in response to a demand, culminated, and passed. Early English was right for the thirteenth century in England; Flamboyant, for the fourteenth century in France: with them we have nothing to do. If we play with them, we are making experiments in archæology, not serving God through His Church. But, when we turn to the last great Gothic of all, the Gothic of William of Wykeham, we turn to the work of our own race, to our own inalienable heritage. Out of the haltings and ventures of three centuries of Englishmen, the bishop of Winchester gathered the good, rejected the bad. A great architect before he took Holy Orders, he saw, by some strange illumination, the goal toward which abbot and monk and mason had been striving. All before had been experimental essays toward national expression, crude often, and always inadequate, but earnest, honorable, consistent. He assimilated it all, fused it in the crucible of his masterly and domineering mind, and produced, at a stroke, that for which generations had patiently labored, — the free, mobile, all-comprehending expression of a religion and a race.

Yet he came too late to make possible the full development of the style he had revealed. Chaos was pending: the foundations of the great civilization of the Middle Ages were being overturned. The Renaissance, Reformation, Rebellion, and Revolution followed, one after the other; and the fabric of mediævalism crumbled to dust. From the day when Henry VIII. began the suppression of the minor monasteries, the doom of Christian architecture was sealed. In a day the work of William of Wykeham came to naught. Thomas Cromwell was succeeded by another of that ilk, he by Wyatt, he by Grimthorpe; and now we find but the shattered fragments of the greatest architectural manifestation England had ever given to the world.

We are working toward a restoration of much that was cast down, though, as we find now, not utterly destroyed. The spirit that is returning to the Church demands expression. We are restoring a theological, doctrinal, and administrative continuity; and we must fitly express this in structural form. This happened in England when the Oxford movement found the Pugins ready to serve the Church with perfect service. The rehabilitation of the churches went hand in hand with the rehabitation of the Church, and it continues unimpeded to this day. The Church in America must emulate the Church in England; and it is nothing short of a solemn duty that urges her to take such action as will result in ending forever the present artistic chaos, substituting in place thereof consistency and unity.

And, if she does this, if she realizes the power of art in her service as a vast agency for good of every kind, if she strives to be outwardly what she has been in the past, if she comes to stand before the world united, consistent, dominating in her material forms, more will follow than merely creditable architecture. At present we flounder in a morass of conflicting systems of art: civil society cannot aid us, for it is equally mired in confusion; the Roman Church is helpless, chained hand and foot by utter artistic depravity, ignorance, and self-satisfaction. We alone cherish the flickering fire that has miraculously been preserved to our hands. The opportunity is era-making. Shall we let it pass?

In Chapter Nine I suggested the possibility of corporate action on the part of the Church toward the determination of a single course of procedure for the immediate future. I believe the gain quite worth the trouble and the cost. If, in connection with some triennial convention, a conference could be held where the whole question of art in its relation to the Church could be thoroughly discussed by the clerical and lay members of the convention, together with church architects from America and England, I believe that the result would be incalculable in its benefits.

Art and religion cannot be dissociated without mutual loss, for in its highest estate the former is but the perfect expression of the latter. The time has surely come for the restoration of the old interdependence, and this would very certainly be effected by such a conference as I have suggested.

Nor should this possible conference confine itself to a consideration of architecture alone: religious painting, decoration, church music, sculpture, metal work, embroidery, all these things might well be considered; and all would be worthy, for all are but certain of the means whereby we try to glorify God and honor the Church He created.

And I am very sure that in point of architecture one decision would be reached unanimously, and that the decision to take up the architectural life of the Church where it was severed in the sixteenth century, and carry to its logical and glorious development the work begun by William of Wykeham, bishop of Winchester. The Church would easily come to see the wrong and the harm of following farther our present chaotic methods. Romanesque and Colonial, Italian and French Renaissance, the early Gothic of France and Germany, Spain and England, would be abandoned; and we should take up once more the great and unfinished style that in the fifteenth century came to express with matchless delicacy all the many and varied qualities of English civilization. On this strong stock would be grafted all of the beauty that could be gathered from the architectural styles of the world. As we have received and assimilated the blood of many nations, making ourselves a mighty and dominant people, so should we assimilate the qualities of their art, grafting on the vigorous stem offshoots from many lands; but, through the whole marvellous growth that would then be possible, would persist in enduring strength the vigorous, vital principle of Christian and English civilization.

10-C

THE BORROWER WILL BE CHARGED
THE COST OF OVERDUE NOTIFICATION
IF THIS BOOK IS NOT RETURNED TO
THE LIBRARY ON OR BEFORE THE LAST
DATE STAMPED BELOW.

JAN 2 7 1981

FINE ARTS
MAR 0 2 2005
BOOK DUE
CANCELLED

FINE ARTS
JUN 1 5 1996
FINE ARTS
FEB 0 2 2005
AUG 2 5 2004
CANCELLED
BOOK DUE

Lightning Source UK Ltd.
Milton Keynes UK
UKHW022253100123
415145UK00005B/81

9 781012 957896